Neelkanth

The Story of a Dream

Mario Perera

Laetitia Buczaczer

Books For All

Delhi

First Published 2014

ISBN 13: 978-81-7386-304-2
ISBN 10: 81-7386-304-0

Published By
Books For All
A-6, Second Floor, Nimri Commercial Centre,
Ashok Vihar Phase-4, Delhi - 110 052 (India)
Tel.: +91 11 2730 2453 Fax: 011 4706 1936
website: www.Lppindia.com
e-mail: info@Lppindia.com

Printed At
D K Fine Art Press P Ltd.
Delhi-110052

PRINTED IN INDIA

Contents

Chapter 1 The Departure 7
Chapter 2 Meeting With a Friend 13
Chapter 3 A Word of Advice 17
Chapter 4 The Apparition 21
Chapter 5 The Initiation 25
Chapter 6 Rishikesh 29
Chapter 7 Questions Seeking Answers 33
Chapter 8 A Deepening Understanding 39
Chapter 9 Uttarakhand: Land of the Gods 45
Chapter 10 The Mystery of Myths 47
Chapter 11 Multiplicity and Sameness 49
Chapter 12 Temples and Statues 55
Chapter 13 Gods 59
Chapter 14 An Encounter With Shiva 63
Chapter 15 Dreams and Myths 69
Chapter 16 An Undying Past 75
Chapter 17 Dream State and Awakened State 79
Chapter 18 Samadhi 83
Chapter 19 Neelkanth 89
Chapter 20 Living With the Ganges 93
Chapter 21 Maya 95
Chapter 22 An Experience of Death 99

Chapter 23 Phantoms of Memory 105
Chapter 24 Recalled to Life 111
Chapter 25 A Joyful Reunion 115
Chapter 26 Unanswered Questions 119
Chapter 27 A Review of Life 125
Chapter 28 Final Revelation of God 135
Chapter 29 The Curtain Falls 139

This book is dedicated

to

Maxence Neelkanth

Chapter 1

The Departure

That night he could not find sleep. His mind was heavy and preponderantly sad. His past was refusing to die. It continued to assail him. The paramount question that cropped up time and again before him was: *have I done my duty by all my dependants*? Much as he tried to evoke the positives in this regard, the final sentiments that gnawed at his heart were those of remorse and regret. The balance weighed heavily on that side. He recalled how a great religious sage had described life as 'suffering'. The 'could have' and the 'should have' heavily outweighed the rest. Whatever be the glow that life had brought him, the shadow of what he had left undone in his personal commitments to his family especially to his parents, made the debit side of his life to surface continually in his mind. The measure was once again not an objective one. He even wondered if the word 'objective' had any sense at all. It was finally a case of his self measuring up to its successes and failures and pining for what could have been but had not been.

Once again he was struck by the imbalances in the scales of measurement of personal life. When he was young the tilt was towards the future. As he reached the mid way mark the scales seemed well balanced, but from then onwards they took a sharp incline towards the past, an incline that continued relentlessly and inexorably until it would engulf what was practically an entire life.

So as to introduce an unexpected weight in the lopsided awareness of the past, his dreams were conjuring up scenes in which his parents figured prominently. He was blaming himself for not having contributed more towards their well being in their old age. There were a few circumstances in that regard that were a principal source of his nostalgia and sadness. They concerned his aged mother and aged father both of whom who died while under his guardianship.

He recalled that period of time when his mother was confined entirely to bed in a state of partial paralysis. His wife had done her very best in spite of being burdened with family responsibilities, especially her profession and the education of their children. He remembered his mother sleeping alone in the room adjoining theirs. She was fast losing her mind, and engaged in rambling senseless utterances during the greater part of the night. *How would she have reacted if it was I in that state* he was constantly asking himself. *She would have left her bed and slept alongside me, her arms around me, lying awake, listening to me, consoling me and attending personally to my every need. But what did I do for her? I slept in my bed waiting for dawn to break and move on with my life.* A voice did rise in his defense. *Yes, but you had to work the next day, earning for your family and for your mother as well. You could not have broken rest and felt fit the next day*. Yet the finger that pointed in his direction was overwhelming and shut every other consideration out.

And then he thought of his father. He was fast losing his mobility and had heavily taken to alcohol. *I could have been more tender and loving. Drinking had become his weakness but I should have borne it especially knowing as I did that his days were numbered. Yet all I did was to arouse in him a sense of culpability for his failings. I could have massaged his stiffened legs and shown him tenderness and love in very many ways. Now he was gone. I will never again get a chance of making amends.*

****

The reproach his past was leveling against him was his failure to love more. Yes love and love alone was the cure for remorse and regret. Its lack would only leave a heart mortally wounded. He heard the voice of the prophet that defended a common prostitute: *much is forgiven her because she has loved much*. Indeed love is the antidote to sorrow, love is the antidote to suffering. All he was asking from the dream figures of his dead parents was forgiveness. *Yes son*, they would reply. *We forgive. Forgiveness is the quality of parenthood. So total and complete is our forgiveness that we do not even remember the failings in our regard you evoke. If there were any, then we have forgotten them without holding back an ounce of remembrance.* He recalled a banner associated with a divinity which read: *when I forgive I forget.* He also recalled a prayer taught by another religious sage addressed to God: *forgive us our offences as we forgive those who have offended us.* Forgiveness and forgetting were the realities of a new heaven and a new earth. As the prophet said: *Behold, I will create new heavens and a new earth. The former things will not be remembered, nor will they come to mind.*

While remembering is the vital condition of our existence, more so is that of forgetting. In the cycle of birth and rebirth, the self in the process of its exchange of bodies must pass through a sea of forgetfulness. Forgetfulness wipes out all the memory data of past existences completely annulling the process of remembering from one existence to another. Truly one is not really dead until all remembrances of him existing in all the memories of the living are totally obliterated and sent into oblivion. "*Behold, I will create new heavens and a new earth. The former things will not be remembered, nor will they come to mind.*" Those were the conditions of a new heaven and a new earth that former things will not be remembered nor that they come to mind.

****

His thoughts now turned to what was his immediate concern: his family, especially his wife. He was her life. All her concern had been centered around him. His health and well being meant all the world to her. He was her god. He felt afraid that her body would melt in tears and pass away through sheer sorrow. Yet having been born to a profound Hindu family, she was aware that this situation could eventually arise. Every man's life was his and his alone. There would come a time when her man would think about his departure from this world and her predicament would be the same as with a natural death. The difference being that in the latter case he would be dead and no more alive to her. In the former instance he would continue to be alive yet dead to her. In both cases re-finding him would be impossible. She would suffer an unspeakable sorrow. Finally she would accept her situation as inevitable and resign herself to her fate. In his case, his death to his family would have to be instantaneous in theory if not in practice. He would have to die to others by dying first and foremost to himself. Very soon he would receive initiation into the life of a wanderer and would have to leave all that had been his life on a funeral pyre and watch it all being reduced to ashes.

****

Since the day the idea took root in his mind, his wife found him thoughtful, taciturn and melancholic. His attitude reflected on hers as well. Yet they both put up a brave front, trying to hide their fears and anxieties from one another. He felt himself like being tied to two ropes that were pulled in opposite directions. He was sixty-eight with the feeling that anything could arise which could shorten or simply cut off his life span. In any case he was convinced that he was living on borrowed time.

He felt he could not take his leave of his family without informing someone. He decided to tell his children. He went to the home of each of his two daughters and told them of his intention. He informed them of the whereabouts of all official documents concerning his property and their transfers. They went to his wife during her life time and after her to the two children. He reminded them of their duties to their mother. The children had given him their hearing with tearful eyes and made their solemn promise that their mother would always have their affection and their care.

****

When the decisively moment did appear, it was not a bolt from the blues. The psychological build up had been taking place and had served in some measure as a shock absorber. He had his own office room in the house, where he spent most of his time. Whenever it was very late in the night, he slept on the couch in that room. It was there he spent his last night. When he got up in the early hours of the morning he had the uncanny feeling that two eyes were on him. Having gathered his meager belongings, he had quietly tiptoed to the main door and opened it very softly.

As he stepped out, he saw his wife waiting for him. She was sobbing in a controlled manner wiping her tears away with the tail end of her sari. She did not say a word but fell at his feet holding on to them and laying her head on them. He had bent down and fondly touched her head. No words were spoken but her stifled sobs rang louder than the peal of temple bells. Then he had made his way out on to the streets, never again to return. He walked quickly until he turned the nearest corner so as to spare his wife the agony of seeing him go, and himself the knowledge that she was watching him. Once that was done he slowed down his space and stood still for his emotions had got the better of him.

From now on time would never more impose conditions on him. He was free. He had died to his family. Now what remained was that he die to himself. From now on a change of name was vital. It was a vital step in dying to oneself, to change one's name. He knew how vital it was to cleanse his mind of everything and anything that held him back to his past. The biggest stumbling block in achieving that would be his self identity. In that regard his name said it all. By eliminating his name he would lay the foundation to make his mind a clean slate. There would be no more writings on that slate. He would follow the example of the Rishis and be all attentive to the voices that could rise within him having as their source the Invisible. He would hold firm as if he saw the Invisible, dissolving into which was from now on his sole ambition.

As for his future name, he knew that all *sadhus* were called '*baba*'. They also had a first name. What would be his? That, time would tell. From now on he was 'baba' to all. It was a generic name which hardly identified anyone from among that anonymous mass that propped up in his mind at its mention. It was just by that name that he would be addressed. Who and what he had been were henceforth of no consequence. Now his only intention was to leave the city of his home without any delay. He did not want to engage in conversation with anyone who might recognize him. He just wanted to go away. He would meet his life long friend for the last time. That would be the final encounter with any one close and dear to him.

Chapter 2

Meeting With a Friend

As expected his friend was there, his eyes were fixed on the passage of the road on which he would appear. As soon as he came into view the former came towards him, half walking half running and soon he felt his warm embrace. *Have you everything*? his friend asked with a concerned look. He assented with an affirmative nod of his head. They were now seated in the restaurant of the station with two steaming cups of tea in front of them. Soon they were evoking their life together at school, at the university and later in the teaching profession. They touched on their long discussions and the themes that occupied their minds.

We were both inveterate dreamers weren't we? his friend said with a gentle smile. Dreamers we were, and so will we always remain, he had answered placing his hand over that of his friend. I wonder whether dying to my past will obliterate those deep insightful discussions we had regarding the nature of dreams and all else that had a bearing to them, he said. *My friend, no need to recall the when, the where and the what. The more you progress in your new life the more your dream will take flesh making your dream body as real as your physical one. When you finally awaken, which I hope will be in this lifetime, you will realize that you are Pure Awareness, that which you always are. Keep on dreaming my friend, for without dreaming there is no Awakening*. His eyes felt moist on hearing these words. I will miss you he said. *I will never be far away, that is as long as you keep on dreaming*, was what his friend said before adding, *and maybe one night on awakening you might find me.*

His life's obsession had been with 'dreams'. It was not a simple theme, but rather a very complex one. It had repercussions and ramifications. It was essentially connected with equally complex subjects such as time, reality, history and myth. The theme of 'dreams' was a veritable labyrinth into which he could not avoid venturing such was the fascination in which the subject held him. Part of this fascination stemmed from his religious and cultural background. It had later taken on a personal turn and become his major preoccupation. He recalled a near death experience of a friend. He had been asked the question: *Do you remember nothing?* To which he replied: *I remember. I remember seeing a dream world: I remember coming from a dream world as if emerging from a womb.* He recalled what his friend had to say on that subject. *The tomb the surrogate womb is sleep but not the conclusion of the dream.*

The dream state is a symbol of the womb. Life is dominated by the shadow of the womb. That shadow strides behind you in the morning, and rises to meet you in the evening. One leaves the womb to re-enter it. One is haunted by the womb, symbolized by the maternal. Life is conserved and nourished within the mother's womb. The father's role is limited to a few spasmodic contractions that release his seed from his body. The rest, conception, conservation and nourishment take place within the body of the mother. The newly born on being ejected from the mother's womb still remains attached to it by the umbilical cord until separated by outside intervention. Hence the attachment of the child to the body of the mother is by a sentiment which is the psychological counterpart of the umbilical cord. *The child remembers its past, its primordial home the womb, which no present can undo. It is finally the reason why the past supersedes the other segments of time.*

Life is the passage from womb to tomb, the tomb being the surrogate womb. Tomb is the passage from one womb to another womb, the transit bridge being the pyre. The tomb is the end station of life's little duration that once appeared to be but never really was. The tomb, the surrogate womb is sleep but not the conclusion of the dream. Lost in reflection his friend's voice appeared as emerging from another realm.

He tried to gather his thoughts together and put them into a coherent whole. The two pivots of his thought world of the moment were the womb and the tomb. While the womb is synonymous with flesh, the tomb is synonymous with 'dust' which is final destination of all flesh. He pictured himself in a lecture hall full of students and answering their questions. *Why is such importance given to dust in all sacred scriptures*? a student was asking him. He was now answering.

Dust is the most omnipresent element of our lives. It is as ubiquitous as the air. Everything that crumbles and decomposes is reduced to dust. Dust is the playground of the wind. The wind wafts it everywhere. Dust is the omnipresent embodiment of all. All that is, is risen from the dust. All that was, has already been reduced to dust, and all that will be, is on their way to becoming dust. We tread on dust, we are bathed in dust, and breathe dust. It is the most intrusive element of our lives. We live surrounded by dust, hemmed in by dust, composed of dust. Dust is what we are for we are dust.

Chapter 3

A Final Word of Advice

The clock on the restaurant wall struck the hour reminding him of his impending departure. *My time to leave is approaching. I am going to miss your words of wisdom. Please fill the little time that is still left for us to be together. How do you think I should lead my future life? To whom should I go for counsel?* He asked. What he heard was like the rumblings of the Himalayan hills. Go to the sources of the waters. They are all in the hills. The source of water is in the hills. As you walk up stream to reach your goal, in the footholds of the hills, on its slopes, in their crevices and precipices loud gush the waters. But when you reach its source stillness prevails. As the poet said: in my end is my beginning. Our end should therefore be to search the beginning for there as in the end, the noises cease and stillness and silence prevail. The one is the silence of creation while the other is the silence of realization. It is out of this silence born of the utmost past and the farthermost future that Divine Awareness will emerge.

Your task now is to create your own new body and make it your vehicle for your journey towards your final realization. Therefore seek the company of those who live in stillness and silence. They are like the mountain sources of the waters where the water is pure and not contaminated by the impurities it accumulates on the way. There in the stillness, one hears the uninterrupted flow of the formless sound of silence. There one experiences the here and the now where nothing comes and goes, just That THAT IS and so remains. Let your mind draw from those two elements: the still and silent waters and the purificatory fire of the pyre. Let your dreams evoke them as the commencement and realization of your endeavour. These are my parting words.

As he finished uttering these words they heard the train approach. They moved towards the platform together wending their way through the thronging multitude. Then came the final embrace as he felt the arms of his friend wrapped around him with all his warmth and love. The last he saw of him was a waving figure that continued waving until he was lost in the distance. *In your dreams we will meet again and again...constantly draw your inspiration from the still and silent waters and the purifying fire of the pyre.* He was repeating these two sentences to himself as the train sped along: *do not forget, it is the nature of dreams to become flesh... and maybe one night on awakening you might find me*

****

He saw the bustling crowd in the compartment into which he had squeezed himself. They pressed against him on all sides. It was as usual boisterous and noisy. When the train stopped at stations, people got down and others got in as they were wont to do. He thought about the people who got out. Where would they be heading for but home. Most of those who got in too were departing for home. As for him, he had left his own. The word home contained connotations of a life time. From his cradle to the moment he left it never to return, home symbolized warmth, security, possession, and above all, love.

Now all those attributes had suddenly seemed so distant, still receding with every jerk and movement of the train in which he sat. The movement of the train was pushing those attributes into the past, and more and more into it. It was as if his recollections of those attributes were being swallowed up within his memory and it was his task not to resuscitate them. It was as if he was entering into his tomb. The rattling of the train were as many clods of earth that were being heaped upon his coffin.

As his mind began drifting all he was experiencing was a medley of thoughts. The one that assailed him now was that of his future solitude. He recalled the message of a guru: *let him always wander alone, without any companion, in order to attain final liberation, fully understanding that the solitary man who neither forsakes nor is forsaken, gains his end. He shall neither possess a fire, nor a dwelling. He may go to a villager for his appointed time, as a servant waits for the payment of his wages.* His was going to be a solitary journey. He would be alone. Yet while this consciousness of solitude was frightening, it was also exhilarating; untethered from all attachments he would be more himself than ever. He felt enlivened by this new feeling of authenticity. Solitude becomes, more than ever, the arena of heroic self-discovery, a voyage through vast interior realms. To achieve authenticity is to look upon these visions without flinching;

****

He was now seated hemmed in from all sides by the throng. He saw nothing due to the multitude crowding the windows and every other opening towards the exterior. All he heard was the rattling of the train. He was living as in a trance. He saw himself in changing perspectives. At one time he felt that he was walking on a vast beach. The monotonous jostling within the train resembled the waves of remorse and regret that were continually arising from the infinite ocean of the past and beating against the shore. The joys were drowned in those two relentless and merciless waves. But yet again the dream world took over and perspectives changed. He felt he had become the tip of a mountain peak which was resting on the immense landmass below it symbolizing his past. From that peak he was looking into the open sky. Then he felt that snow clad and ice hard peak thawing under the heat of thought and emotion, of remorse and regret.

Now, he felt himself melting into tears which flowed down like rivers. *How could these rivers of tears be turned into waters of joy*? He felt himself gushing in a stormy and emotional manner out of his mind through falls, gorges and ravines. Then become tranquil and gentle he was emerging into the plains. He saw people of all ages, and conditions of life plunging into his waters and bathe in them, shedding their fatigue and coming out renewed and refreshed. He saw his tears of remorse and regret turning into a source of joy for man and beast. He expressed this new found feeling through the word *Anandamayi* or joy. He could only counteract remorse and regret through becoming joy for others.

Whatever brought joy could be nothing else than the spark of divine consciousness calling him to break out of that encirclement as well as out of the cycle of life and death. He had to turn his dream world into a joyous experience. Only through that would he realize that the very ephemeral nature of life was such that regret and remorse had no place in it. From now on his goal would be to encounter joy. *Anandamayi*, *Anandamayi*, his mind cried out, *where are you*?

Chapter 4

The Apparition

And then he felt his eye lids succumbing to their weight. Like a big wave overwhelming him sleep came, drawing him into the realms of silence. But it was only for a moment. He now saw himself seated alongside flowing waters. Eager to have a glimpse of himself he looked into its mirror. What he saw troubled him. It was the figure of a man who had aged beyond recognition. His hair and beard were all white, his face was wrinkled. *Is this what I have become*: he heard himself asking. *Yet it was just like yesterday*.

And then he saw another face looking at him in the mirror of the same waters. It was a woman. *Do not worry my baba*, she was telling him. *Nothing has changed*. Who are you? he asked her. *I am Anandamayi* she replied. Her face brought back memories of his past when he began life as a teacher. It was the face of a student who had been deeply in love with him. You are Maya, he said. *I was Maya, my baba*, she answered, *now I am Anandamayi*. Why have you come, Maya? He asked, ignoring her comment. *I am come to bring you joy, my baba*. I am old now, Maya, he answered with a voice weighed by fatigue. Do you not see my face? *What is age my baba*, she said, unimpressed by his concern. *Look at me, have I aged?* No, he said surprised by the youth of the apparition. *Everything depends on the mirror you look into, my baba. You are looking into the mirror of the waters: it is an impersonal mirror. I am looking into your eyes. Your eyes are the mirror of our love. Look into my eyes baba*, she said, He did as she requested. What he saw of himself was totally different. His wrinkles had gone, so had the whiteness of his hair. It was the face of the young teacher he had been when Maya introduced herself into his life.

****

What is happening to me? he asked in amazement. Then she made ready to go. No he said, do not go. *I must my baba, you will be awake soon. But one night by the light of the moon we will unite. On that night you will call me Anandamayi, and I will never leave you again my baba*, she was saying. Wait he said, but isn't this a dream? *It is dreams that take flesh, my baba* she answered, adding: *I know where you are heading for*. How can that be? he asked. *My baba, since the day I entered your mind, I never left it.*

Baba, my baba, do you remember the promise I made to you? It was a promise full of youthful hopes and in the form of a song that I sang gently in your ear, although you remained stoically non committal. Let me sing it once again for you my baba.

I'll walk beside you through the world today
While dreams and songs and flowers bless your way
I'll look into your eyes and hold your hand
I'll walk beside you through the golden land

I'll walk beside you through the world tonight
Beneath the starry skies ablaze with light
Within your soul love's tender words I'll hide
I'll walk beside you through the eventide

I'll walk beside you through the passing years
Through days of cloud and sunshine, joys and tears
And when the great call comes, the sunset gleams
I'll walk beside you to the land of dreams

Maya, he said with great earnestness in his voice. You belong to my past, the past I will be shedding. *My baba, how can you? Your very life is a construct of your past*. He looked at her questioningly. So she continued. *The clearest proof of what I say will be provided by the Sadhus you will see around you. They smear ash on their bodies to symbolize the death of their past. But will one smearing suffice my baba? The moment that ash wears out, their past appears again. So the smearing will go on and on. You will notice others trying to burn away their past with fire, hoping that the smoke will carry it away. But does it go away my baba? They will light the fire and smoke it away, but it will come back. So the lighting and the smoking will go on and on. What is past and what is present my baba? Wherein lies the difference? It is in the forms and how they are presented to the mind in its many states. The mind, my baba, is the mirror of time.*

Maya had evoked fire, smoke and ash, all elements of the pyre which brought back to him the words of his friend: Let your mind draw from those two elements: the still and silent waters and the fire of the pyre. What is it you are trying to tell me, Maya, he asked in desperation. *Accept the joy your past is offering you on a platter.* In what form will it come to me? He heard himself asking. *The form that will emerge from the ocean of your sub-conscious, my baba. What matters is joy and its fruit.* Maya, he said, you know my past. I have left wife and children to walk on a solitary and lonely road. Knowing all that why do you still follow me? *My baba* she answered back. *The part of the life you lived with open eyes is only the visible tip of the massive invisible iceberg of who you really are. The life you lived comprised customs, conventions, products of circumstances. You were never the creator of those circumstances my baba, you were their creature. The world of open eyes has nothing more to offer you my baba. They can never fill your real and as yet unrealized yearnings embodied in your invisible person. I am your unrealized dream my baba. It is not I who am pursuing you. It is you who are unconsciously calling me up from your formless depths within which I lie. From the depths of your being you are crying out to me my baba. You will not stop doing so until I become flesh and blood.*

He was stunned by this statement and instinctively took a step in her direction. As he did so, he saw a woman advancing towards him holding a little boy against her breast. Maya, he shouted in his sleep, Maya, where are you? Then he felt a hand gently shaking him awake. *We have arrived*, the voice was saying. As he opened his eyes he heard the train grinding to a halt. He had arrived in *Haridwar*. He alighted from the train and boarded a bus to *Rishikesh*.

Chapter 5

The Initiation

Years had passed since he had bid farewell to his past life. As if to stamp a burning seal on it, his thoughts went back to his initiation into *Sannyasi* life. What engrossed him most were the background and the predominant events and elements that constituted the ceremony. It was full of profound contrasts that seemed to rake up the past to its roots. He seemed like a wanderer in a desert where time was as fragile as a mirage.

The space around had been converted into the temple of *Guru Dattatreya*, the primordial *Yogi* and patron of all ascetics. The hall was very dark and several enclosures had been erected within. In each enclosure the future disciples, their heads fully shaved with bodies totally bare except for the semblance of a loin cloth, sat in a circle around their guru and his assistants. In the middle of each enclosure a funeral pyre had been erected. What was taking place was a cremation. The corpse on the pyre had no identity of itself but of that of all claiming entry into sannyasi state. In other words each and everyone aspiring to that way of life was assisting at his own cremation.

Everything appeared more as a dream than reality. Indeed it went beyond the realm of the dream, it appeared totally unreal. To add to that effect the ceremony began with the salutation of the mother goddess of illusion, *Maya Devi*. What was being reenacted was a primordial myth. The underlying assumption was the importance of truth whatever be the form in which it was brought to mind, whether reality, irreality, dream or the awakened state. They were all offshoots of the transcendental truth, the truth inaccessible to reason. The ocean of illusion was about to be churned for the extraction of the elixir of immortality.

Then the fire ceremony began. The spark that fired and lit the ceremony was obtained from the primordial fire kept alive in the hearth of the temple. The fire *Thali* made its way around the hall as if piercing the dark spaces and the pyres were lit up and set ablaze. The whole hall seemed to vanish behind a smoke screen. The hazy smoky air emanated from the burning wood, straw, incense, and combined with the thicker, much more pungent and penetrative smell of burning flesh. Illusion had thrown its veil over every semblance of reality. It was in this eerie atmosphere that the candidates were being proposed for entry into the *sanniyasi* life.

And then the *Shiva* mantras vibrated through the hall in unending waves of frenetic fervor. The crowd was shouting iself hoarse with: *Nama Shivaya nama Shiva, hare hare bole nama Shiva. Rameshvara Shiva Rameshvara, hare hare bole nama Shiva.* The first glimmer of light was piercing the mortuary shroud of smoke that had engulfed the living and the dead. It seemed now that *Shiva* had taken his place among his entourage descending from his lofty Himalayan abode at the bequest of his servants. Cries of *Hara Hara Mahadev* and *Jai Shiva Shankar* rent the air like powerful winds whipping up the blazing fires of the pyres that were reducing the illusion of life and death to ashes. It was as if mother earth had burst asunder as would a volcano revealing the divine flame that lay within her womb.

The *Mahadev* that appeared through the flame was the destroyer of illusion. The dark night of ignorance was being lit by the light of Divine Consciousness. The delusionary workings of the senses were being laid bare as the pure light of Awareness exploded the illusion of self and its worlds.

The occupants of the hall were led into the experience of death to the self now identified with the lifeless bodies being consumed in the pyres. The awareness that filled the hall was: *no, I am not that, I am the Immortal Self, the Eternal One.* The shroud of mortality had been torn asunder and the mantle of immortality had taken its place.

****

In conformity with the nature of the event, those present in the hall were more apparitions than real. Some were vividly decorated with colours, others daubed with ash from the crematoriums – using their body as a canvas for their beliefs. Ochres and roans and rusts mingled with the pervasive swirl of white and grey ash. The visual was the most powerful aspect of the sensory world. It was the visual which was being made use of by these holy men to reveal and transmit a body of spiritual heritage unprecedented in the annals of religious history. Their naked bodies were a reminder of the nakedness of the self in the eyes of divine awareness. The ash was a reminder of the earthly destiny of all created beings. Their wild appearance was a reminder of the illusory nature of earthly beauty, charm and elegance. Their bodies with their powerful symbolism were the all important pages from the divine scriptures. They were the canvas on which the divine painter rendered the macrocosm visible and tangible.

It was a depiction of the universe as *maya* or illusion. But even more, it served as a gravitational force more powerful than earthly attractions, to draw observers from the realm of the transitory and ephemeral to the timeless divine beyond body and form. What the body of each apparition embodied and proclaimed was the egoless state to which conventional standards of society with its complex hierarchy, taboos and customs would no longer be applicable.

The final words of the guru as his wrapped the *dhoti* around each of them were: *This final gift is your protection and sheltering of Mother Earth. It is the color of her soil, ochre, her life-blood. See how long this fine cloth is when unfolded? It is a flag marking that you are in her hands, and that you are on the Path. For you there is no more a past, and no more a future, just an eternal unending NOW. Time has lost its hold on you.*

The earth he now trod would never again be something alien or strange. It was now someone: it was his mother. And now she was talking to him. *Son, it is not you who henceforth takes me along with you, but I who take you along within me. It is I who carries you, feeds you, nourishes you, maintains you and sustains you. Your journey is with me, from my womb of darkness and illusion to the light of reality and truth. I am the filament that encapsulates the air of breath within me, that you are. The day realization dawns in you as to your true nature, that day my womb will open and release you into the ONE that you unknowingly are and had always been.*

Chapter 6

Rishikesh

His initiation into sannyasi life began almost immediately on his arrival in *Rishikesh*. On reaching the place he solemnly proclaimed: *This is where my journey has led me. My teachers will be the still and silent waters and the purificatory fire of the pyre. My language will be the sound of silence.*

He woke up early like the other *sadhus* and headed first for the Ganges for his personal purification rituals. After the bath and washing clothes, he regained the rocky ledges overlooking the river and sat recollecting his thoughts. Then he proceeded to the nearest alms center and drank a cup of tea served in a small earthen bowl. After that he felt free to organize himself as he wished. He had decided not to follow the path laid down by a specific guru, but to find his way as best as he could.

The first months of separation from his family and his social milieu weighed heavily on him. It all came back all the time like successive waves on an ocean of memories day and night. He had found an abandoned tent on the banks of the Ganges where he spent his nights. But sleep did not come as expected. He was awakened at dead of night by phantom like figures representing family members and close acquaintances. The most persistent of the figures tormenting his dreams was that of his wife, entreating him to return, drawing his attention to her solitude and overwhelming sorrow. He tried to shake off those recollections by walking incessantly, bare footed, a single saffron cloth wrapped around his waist. He walked so fast as to outdo his memories that he disappeared from the view of passers-by as quickly as he appeared. The nights were dark and the roads were barely lit up but his ghost like phenomenon impressed regular onlookers who soon began referring to him as 'Ganga Baba', so elusive he was like the waters of the sacred river. When day broke he was often still awake but tired and worn out by his nocturnal adventures.

Then there were the physical hardships. Living in a battered makeshift tent involved great sacrifices. He had no bedding to sleep on, was assailed by myriad mosquitoes and was in such poverty he could not procure the needs of a life style well below poverty level. Even the food he found to be so tasteless and so unpalatable. He was constantly falling sick with the commonest ailments. Once someone remarked that he appeared to be suffering from jaundice, but the remark had no serious impact as he could no more distinguish between one physical state and another. Furthermore he did not even known how he looked like having no mirror to look into and no desire to do so either. He had indeed suffered from dysentery, hepatitis, and was now told he had jaundice. All he knew was that whatever be it that he had, he survived.

Amidst all this the silver lining in this dark night he was traversing was that life had still the glimmerings of the heaven he had left everything for. He walked as if he saw the undying, and death had no place in his mind. He was striving to experience *Samadhi* (enlightenment) in a world in which *maya* (illusion) and *moksha* (liberation) constituted the two scales of the balance.

****

Progressively his resistance to hardships increased and the intensity of his memories subsided while peace began returning to his tormented mind. He searched for a distraction which would take his mind off his past and the travails of everyday life while enlightening him about his present condition. So it was that he began to show eagerness to know as much as he could of the life style of the other ascetics.

He knew that the term *Sadhu* had vast interpretations among his countrymen. The word designated holy men, derelicts, madmen, charlatans, wanderers, mystics and yogis. He remembered the words of *Krishna* to *Arjuna*: *I am all that you think, all that you say. Everything hangs on me like pearls on a thread. I am the earth's scent and the fire's heat. I am appearance and disappearance. I am the trickster's hoax. I am the radiance of all that shines. I am time grown old.* Who else but renunciates would symbolize the crucible of the timeless in which time melts away? No wonder then that the overall sentiments that people entertained in their regard was one of awe and reverence. They had renounced all.

Chapter 7

Questions Seeking Answers

Nevertheless the question had to be asked: *who were they*? Their lives were considered as merging with the mists of the past and emerging from the beginning. At the same time they were thought of as disappearing into and uniting with the horizons of the future. With a beginning that touched the end, all that that lay in between in the form of time and space was totally eclipsed and invalidated. Their lives evolved in the 'here and now' devoid of all temporal and spatial connotations. The answer to the question *who are you*? could only be: *I am one divested of a past.* As for the question where are you going? they could only answer: *Where can I go? I am here, where I always was and always will be. I am one who is here and now. In me the mortal and the immortal, the finite and the infinite, the temporal and the eternal, life, death and rebirth coexist, like imperceptibly overlapping seasons of nature, portrayed on the one virtual landscape which is my body.*

They lived in unbounded liberty, a liberty beyond the pale of conventional life and its standards and parameters. They enjoyed the freedom of the divine. They were gods that walk the earth living of the love, the reverence and the homage paid to them by mortals. They transformed hard reality into fluid dreams, history into myths. They were literally time machines without frontiers, without confines. They were paths from here to eternity. In them earth and heaven were so fused that where one ended and the other began no mind could tell. They were living answers to the mysteries of life, of death and rebirth. They represented the all pervading and all embracing Divine Awareness. In it nothing began, nothing ended but all transpired within an ever enduring ageless commencement. Each one could have been expected to say with the great sage of *Arunachala* on the verge of dying: *they say I am dying, that I am going away. But where should I go? I am here.*

****

The more he got to know the renunciates his knowledge turned back to him as a question. *What was it that animated the minds of these men*? The answers to that question were many though not easy to elicit. Yet there seemed to be a thread that found its way through all the responses his mind formulated. They all seemed to want to jettison whatever trace of a personal identity that still had a hold on their mind. It was as if they were straining to realize their new birth. He felt as though the symbolic death and cremation enacted during the initiation ceremony into sannyasi life was proving insufficient for that purpose. He felt the words of Maya vibrate within him: *They smear ash on their bodies to symbolize the death of their past. But will one smearing suffice my baba? The moment that ash wears out, their past appears again. So the smearing will go on and on. You will notice others trying to burn away their past with fire, hoping that the smoke will carry it away. But does it go away my baba? They will light the fire and smoke it away, but it will come back. So the lighting and the smoking will will go on and on. What is past and what is present my baba? Wherein lies the difference? It is in the forms and how they are presented to the mind in its many states. The mind, my baba, is the mirror of time.*

To die to their past the holy men would all have to deal with an ineluctable condition: one's identity or the 'I am' feeling. It was the thread that wove the tapestry of body and mind. Getting rid of it would also mean releasing one's hold on one's body and mind which precisely was the aim and goal of the renouncer's life. It was like making an ice rock hard mountain peak thaw and flow out as water.

It was well known to him that masks and other camouflage served the purpose of personality change. What was a face, what was a body but a mask worn by the divine in his peregrinations through time? The endeavour of the *sadhus* clearly pointed in that direction. First the highly imaginative make up of their hair and their beards, and then the colourings on their bodies. Naturally each gave full vent to personal initiatives in giving expression to their ideas and ideologies.

The paths to Divine Awareness were multifarious, as illustrated by the many sects to which the holy men belonged. Through such adherences they were giving free rein to the most secret and undisclosed urges and tendencies of their minds and bodies, even though they could seem abhorrent to the uninitiated. They were thereby professing the freedom of the divine, a freedom that lies hidden from the reaches of the conventional mind. That freedom only proclaimed the greatness of God and the inscrutable nature of his ways. No stone would be left unturned in their search of the Hidden One. All paths would be explored to the very end. They were the torch bearers of humanity. That torch would light up every hidden recess and cavern of the mind, it would venture where even angels fear to tread. Their hearts had no fear, and they would dare to enter and explore where the bravest would desist. Each and every one of them could have said with the poet: *the woods are lovely dark and deep but I have promises to keep, and miles to go before I sleep.*

What about chillum smokers? asked a voice intruding into his thoughts. He recalled the view point Maya had proffered during their meeting in the train. The three elements that stood out from her statement were: fire, smoke and ash, all symbols of the pyre, the bridge between two wombs, the passage of forgetfulness and oblivion. He thought he must pose that question to the god of the ascetics, *Guru Dattatreya.* Lord Guru he said, how do you reconcile this practice with the goals of the renunciates? Then he heard the Lord reply: *That practice for those living in the realm of uninhibited liberties and freedom is itself a path to the hidden cavern within their minds that conceal the Ineffable. It is a vehicle for some, for their journey into the ocean of the formless and the anonymous. No path would remain unexplored and no stone would remain unturned in that endeavour.* He recalled the words of the Latin poet: nihil humanum mihi alienum – nothing human is alien to me. Guru Dattatreya continued his explanation: *The chillum smoking sadhus elevated a way of life that society looked down on to the sphere of the sublime. They transformed a derogatory practice into a form of worship. Symbols and meanings which conventional society considered as worthy and respectable, they brought to naught in a blaze of fire. The derision, scorn and ignominy of society they blew away in smoke. The values of such a society they reduced to ash in a show of consummate disdain.*

But behind all this conspicuous activity lay a silent endeavour, that of trying to weave for themselves a garb of anonymity. Behind the smudge and camouflage of colour and riggings each was trying to merge his body with that of the other in order that all would be seen for what they really were: ONE. That struggle primarily involved fending off the invasion of the senses which was far from over.

****

As this thought took possession of him he felt himself being wafted to the middle of the battle field of *Kurukshetra*. As the dream made its way he suddenly felt his body being donned with the armoury and weapons of a warrior. He was being transformed into *Arjuna*. His five senses which he now visualized as the five horses pulling the chariot of his self were engaged in a frenetic struggle to break loose from the reins he held in his hands. The war he was waging was against the objects of these senses which were trying to subjugate and enslave him. He realized that the battle field of *Kurukshetra* was his mind. Then he felt a human form standing beside him whom he immediately recognized as being *Krishna*.

Lord, he said, *I need your guidance. But I cannot hear you above the din and clatter of my senses. Can you help me, Lord*? I cannot tame your senses for you. That you must do, was *Krishna*'s reply. Your senses are continuously exposed to their objects and continuously assailed by them. Your senses are like these five turbulent horses. Do you see how restless they are? Once your mind yields to their agitation you are lost in the objects of these senses as in a labyrinth without issue, and you drift away from me into the hands of the hordes of mara aligned against you on the battlefield of life. *But maya has clouded my reason, Lord. How can I fight these hordes of mara? The objects of my senses appear before me as hands that turn the wheel of my life, the one and only life that I know of. I feel incapable of controlling them. I feel compelled to go along*. The mind clouded by maya is chained to the wheel of mara and subjected to recurrent death and rebirth with its incessant passage from the womb to the tomb with the pyre as the bridge between the two. You must fight this tyranny of the senses and attune your mind to the deathless Self within you and that you are. Indeed be still and in that deafening silence you will know that you are God. Warrior stand up and fight. I will drive your chariot, but the fight is entirely in your hands. I cannot fight that battle for you.

That thick layer of ash on his body was a perpetual reminder that: *the kingdom of the mind is no more than a construct of the senses and their fleeting impressions. It is sifting sand. One's self is the castle built on it. The glue that makes the ensemble seem to hold is only a feeling, that of the 'self'* The goal of the renunciate was just to unburden himself of it, just let go of it and feel the surge of joy, ecstasy and bliss. But letting go of it would not be easy. So many realms had merged to constitute his human person epitomized in the 'self'. He was a veritable 'sangam' of rivers that had combined to continue their onward flow under one identity.

Full deliverance would only come when smoke issuing from the fire of the pyre vanishes into thin air and the ash that smears the site of the pyre disintegrates into dust for ever. There must be nothing left to re-gather. He had a battle on his hands to be waged. Kurukshetra was not just a myth, it was truth and the voice of Krishna was still ringing through the mists of his mind: *I will drive your chariot, but the fight is entirely in your hands.*

Chaper 8

A Deepening Understanding

His initiation to a life of renunciation could not have been better than by learning from those who had already renounced. Sitting among other renunciates and listening to them talk afforded him a wealth of knowledge of their way of life. Whenever the question of pilgrimages arose, all places renouncers talked about traveling from and heading to, were sites which indicated the focal points of their lives. Many pilgrimage sites were famous because they marked a unique geographical phenomenon: the source of a river, for example at *Gangotri*, or the exact point where plains turned into mountainous foothills, for example in *Haridwar*. They invariably became the location of a shrine to which both lay pilgrims and sadhus traveled for blessings. The sacred geographical space came first, their association with sacred events came next and the commemorative temple came after.

These spots were sacred ground. They drew a pilgrim's attention to the wonders of landscape, the vastness of nature, and the way individual places are connected to one another through the flow of water or the undulating surface of the earth. Their geographical qualitics transformed these pilgrimage locations into sites of particular mythical events or activities in the lives of deities in one or other of their many incarnations. Although engaged in a purely personal endeavour, this collective preoccupation with mythical space created links between disparate places and served as a mystic thread that each renunciate held in his hand giving them a sense of unity and communion. Distanced from chronological time and space it was the mythical and the mythological that animated their lives and dreams. One of the highest points of convergence of time and eternity was the *Kumbh Mela*.

****

The *kumbh* lies in the deepest recesses of the subconscious mind: so deep in its recess that it effaces the dividing line between time and eternity. It is at the very origin of the mythical world with its shimmering light of creation in the womb of life. The *kumbh* very appropriately means 'pot' of clay which is circular in form molded in the hands of the divine potter. The Divine molder, by his act of molding the pot of cosmic life reveals himself as *maya.* It is within the pot that unfolds the mystery of creation and deliverance.

How did this idea come into my head? asked his inquisitive mind. How can the pot, the *kumbh* be the key to the mystery of creation and deliverance? The silence that greeted this question now turned into sound, and the sound became a voice. *Let us consider the pot in the hands of its maker. Where would its opening point to?* To its maker, he heard himself replying. *To the source of the Divine breath,* the voice said. *That breath is the source of creation. That breath condenses into water, and water hardens and becomes earth. In the inverse order in the light of Divine awareness, the earth would liquefy become water and water would vapourize into breath and return creation to its maker.* The argument seemed perfectly logical. Now, the voice continued, *how would the same pot act when in the inverted form in the hands of maya?* The inverted form of the pot would be the form of the womb, he said. *Quite true,* the voice confirmed, *the womb of maya. Now let us consider the actions and reactions of the pot in that inverted form. The breath of the Divine transformed into water would flow out. Thus time would be formed. The hardening of earth would engender the space element. Life would then be endowed with all requisites for its illusory stability, continuity and interconnectedness. It would now be manifest as the one and the many eclipsing the ONE in the many. The one divine awareness would seemingly multiply into many individual consciousnesses. From now on the ONE would seem as being the many. The return to the divine has necessarily to be through the waters. It is in the water within the divine mold, the pot, that the maker's breath lies encapsulated. That divine breath is the amrit, the elixir of immorality. It is finally a question of how the pot is held: towards the maker or away from him.* The majestic teaching left him in a trance. Then his lips moved with reverence and formulated the phrase: *Om jai Gange Mata.*

****

Both gods and demons were born out of the living waters of the pot of life. The difference lay in what Enlightenment meant to them. For the gods, it meant the pot with its opening pointing towards the face of God. For the demons, it meant the pot as the womb of maya. For the former life became the search of the truth of their true Self, the ONE. For the latter it meant clutching on to their individualized nature as one among the many. It meant the false eternity of permanence in the unending world of maya, the great illusion. It meant the illusion of the unending continuity and permanence of life with its passage between the womb and the tomb over the fire of the pyre. It meant taking what is transient as permanent; and what is suffering as happiness.

Then the mighty god *Ram* took form in his imagination. He spoke. *Lost in the life of illusion and beset with the fear of death, both gods and demons found themselves in the same predicament. They both needed a guarantee of eternity and immortality conceived by the ones and the others according to the measure of their minds. So they agreed to churn the waters, now appearing as the milky ocean, at the bottom of which lay the elixir of immortality, the divine amrit. To that end they translocated a mythical mountain Madura into the ocean, wound the mythical serpent Vasuki around it.*

Now appeared the multi headed demon king *Ravana*. He addressed reproaches to *Ram*. From the beginning your endeavour was to cheat us. First you entrusted to us the head of Vasuki with its propensity to vomit its venom, while you held on to its tail. Your deceptions continued all the way. *Rama* brushed aside the charge. *Deceit*, he said *is the language of illusion. In the world of maya the truth undergoes distortions. Without a discerning mind you cannot see the difference.* He then continued. *Tugging the serpent from both ends in rotational movements we stirred and agitated the ocean making it foam and yield its precious liquid.*

Finally the *amrit* was extracted. From then gods and demons chase each other over inconceivable eons of time and inconceivable expanses of space trying to wrest the elixir from the hands of each other. Their exploits were recounted in thousands of episodes. The *Kumbh Mela* heralds the final victory of the gods. On that occasion the gods, merging in the bodies of the renunciates assure and guarantee the devotees of their final success, and impart to them their blessings. For the devotees who participated in those events, they were also a unique opportunity to enjoy the dharshan of the saints and sages thronging around Mother Ganges in a manifestation of filial love, devotion and solidarity.

Mother Ganges is the life blood of the Land of the Gods. His mind was still full of the pot of creation in the hands of the divine molder. Now his mind was centered on the Ganges and he wanted to know her story. Tell me your story, Mother, he asked the sacred river seated on the lowermost step of the ghat which was his home. *Son*, she replied, *you just learned of the ever enduring conflict between the gods and the demons for the possession of the divine 'amrit', the nectar of immortality. My story is an essential part of that rivalry. I was also born in a pot, the water pot or kamandulla Brahma used to wash his feet. I the delight and the pleasure of the heavens later reincarnated as a river. My descent on earth was the result of penances and austerities of King Bhagiratha with intent to purify the ashes of his brothers and obtain their liberation. His penances were so intense and so earnest they melted the heart of Shiva who accepted to break the impact of my fall with the matted locks of his hair. I, the water of the divine pot now turned river, am the source of purification and liberation of all. I, the water which once washed the divine feet of Brahma, now serve as the waters in which all bodies, human and animal plunge and emerge purified of their sins, become claimants of the divine amrit.*

Mother, he said awe struck by this narrative; you, the water that filled that pot, are the divine breath condensed into liquid form. That breath, the amrit, the elixir of immortality, now flows through the land of the gods as our mother, as Mother Ganga. Mother, you are the eternal celestial waters: you are the milky ocean, the container of the divine amrit. Now, just as then, gods and demons personified in the human forms that we are, plunge into you and churn your waters to extract from your womb the guarantee of immortality. And now just as then, we pursue each other, we the gods and demons, to snatch that guarantee in the form of the life giving drops, each with his own idea of that promise. For the gods among us, that promise will be eternally fulfilled the day we realize and abide in the Divine Awareness of our Real Self. As for the demons among us, they will achieve that promise differently, through the illusory eternity and immortality of unending existences within the interminable cycle of birth, death and rebirth.

Mother,I now understand why the Lord of life and death has chosen your ice clad form, to be the form of his Himalayan abodes. I understand now why you assume the form of the dancing Lord, the Nataraja, on your descent into the plains, assuming his role as the passage from death to immortality.

Chapter 9

Uttarakhand:Land of the Gods

He had always wanted that his life as a renouncer be spent in *Uttarakhand*, the land of pilgrimages and of saints. He recalled how some of the drops of the divine amrit had fallen on the land he had chosen for his new life: the land with the greatest concentration of pilgrimage destinations and the sources of the sacred rivers. It was also the greatest region of the confluence of rivers. It is especially the region where the Ganges begins, takes form, and makes its way to the plains of India. This land bore the footsteps of the greatest number of pilgrims. It was a land kneaded by the footsteps of saints and pilgrims, *kneading the earth like churning the ocean, in search of the nectar of immortality*.

Whenever he trod this sacred ground he recalled how the divine addressed a prophet of old telling him: *Remove your shoes for the place you stand on is holy*. It was common belief that gods walked the earth. The soil on which he trod had borne the print and the weight of such gods. But what were gods but the ONE become the many? The soil he trod was holy having being consecrated by the footsteps of myriads of saints who abided in the Self, as the fount of holiness. Realization was dawning on him that mother earth was holy, that it was replete with the awareness of the divine. He realized that each step he took on this holy ground was a call to empty his self and merge with the many who had abandoned their personal identity in the light of Divine Awareness. His life was being filled with meaning. Realization was dawning that the path and the destination were really one. There was no starting point and a final tape to breast. Divine Awareness could explode within him at any step he took. That step would be the prayag where the tributaries and confluents of temporal and the eternal met and fused together.

On his way upwards he saw how all the rivers that flowed downwards towards *Rishikesh*, met and mixed with the Ganges: the *Bhagirathi* coming from beyond the *Gaumukh* at *Deoprayag*, the *Mandakini* coming down from *Kedernath* and the *Alaknanda* from *Badrinath* at *Rudraprayag*. It was from *Deoprayag* onwards that the sacred river flowed as the Ganges. Just as the confluences, so too his own steps merged with those of the past and those to come. This was a transforming experience that stirred him to the depths of his being and he waited for nightfall to share his feelings with Mother Ganga.

Mother, he said, at each step I take I hear the echoes of many. *Do you remember your day of initiation into the sannyasi life?* Mother was asking him. I do Mother, he answered. *Do you remember what Mother Earth told you about your relationship with her?* was her next question. He now recalled what he had heard: it was not he who would from now on be taking her along with him, it was she who would take him within her. It was she who was carrying him. *You have only the sensation of moving*, she reminded him, *it is Mother Earth that carries you in her womb. You are a hiker on memory trail. The sound of each footstep you seem to take reverberates with the echo of the many. They are all living memories that mother earth so fondly conserves and revives. It is like a human mother turning the pages of the album of her heart in which all her children are enshrined. Her remembrance of one reverberates with the remembrances of the many.* I am confused, Mother, how is all that possible? *I will tell you. The ONE, the SELF that you are is in all you think, you say, you see, you touch and hear. The more you divest yourself of your self, the less you become one among many, and the more you become the ONE in all. Then your step becomes one, you see one, you hear one, you touch one, and you become ONE. Indeed you weren't anything else at any time but ONE.* Tat tvam asi – thou art THAT.

Chapter 10

The Mystery of Myths

Abiding in the stillness of the SELF was what the saintly *rishis* had experienced in their state of *Samadhi* or merging with Absolute Awareness. The experience of *Samadhi* was removed from the sphere of historical narratives. It had no chronology. It did not depend on time and space. How can one reveal the content of such an experience as a calendar event with dates and places as supports? How then can an experience of Infinity, of Immortality and of Eternity be handed down? How else but by enlightening narratives or stories called myths? These stories afforded penetrative insights about man and God devoid of the additives of time and space. It was on myths that the entire belief system of his people stood. Myths were part and parcel of the cyclic view of life. They were like unending waves of an eternal ocean.

He mind dwelt on his visit to the *Mana* village in *Badrinath* famous for *Vyas* rock cave where *Vyas Maharishi* dictated his famous great epic of *Mahabharata* to Lord *Ganesh*. That scene propped up before his eyes and came alive. He heard the *Maharishi* say: *the Mahabharatha is the embodiment of the word myth. It is one and many. It seems to begin and end, but it has neither a beginning nor an end. There are hundreds of Mahabharatas, hundreds of different manuscripts and innumerable oral versions making it impossible to make an accurate calculation of the number of its verses. The Mahabharata is not contained in a text; the story is there to be picked up and found, salvaged as anonymous treasure from the ocean of story.*

As an ascetic wanderer the purpose of his life was to pick up and find the story of his life and existence, salvaging it as anonymous treasure from the ocean of story. That ocean of story for him was his dream world which was also the seed bed of myth.

Chapter 11

Multiplicity and Sameness

Many questions assailed him. On such occasions the advice of his friend invaded his mind as the golden rule to follow: *constantly draw your inspiration from the purifying fire of the pyre.* On that pyre the latest vehicle of his self would be consumed leaving behind little scatterings of whitish ash that survived the flames. Whatever there remained of consciousness was akin to the ash of a hearth likened to the latent energy within the womb. It was there that the throb of life would be felt once more: the manifestation of the divine 'amrit' in the miniature milky ocean that was the maternal womb. His mind like an erased slate would emerge within a woman's womb and then the travail of birth towards self identification begins. That mind within the womb would still be darkness and devoid of an identity which would grow in unison with the body. He was an absence groping his way unconsciously towards becoming a presence incorporated in a new body. He realized the vital role played by the body in the awakening of his self consciousness.

The self that was witnessing the happenings knew that he, as he had known himself to be, had disappeared into oblivion. His previous life with its feelings, emotions, thoughts, memory and imagination had been effaced with his entire human network and connections. His past was as good as non-existent. His previous world had ceased to exist. Yet his mind, one and the same by its re-emergence as 'self' through a re-created body was awakening into a totally different network of relationships, in a different framework of time and space. He would never know whether the world of his present birth was the same as the previous. He would not know himself as any other but the one incorporated in that particular body. He had to take in his new world and experience it as it was, for what seemed to him to be, the first and the only one. *Who, when and where could I have been when the only self I know and could ever know is that of my actual identity?*

****

Grappling with this problem without respite he sank into a reverie amidst the din and clatter of the life around him. *How does one explain this astounding multiplicity yet the persisting sameness of the renunciates around me?* The multiplicity presented them as many but striking similarities seemed to suggest that their identities overlapped in spite of their show of diversity. I am confronted on a daily basis with the faces of countless *sadhus*, many old and hoary daubed in ritualistic paint with matted locks of long hair, he muttered to himself. I watch them coming towards me, walking alongside me, seated or sleeping side by side with me. Their facial make up, their body colourings, their voices, gaits, actions and reactions were of distinct individuals. But what the mind perceived was an anonymous uniform mass. *So it is also with the waves of the ocean. They all looked like ever changing blotches of forms and glimmerings but the underlining feature of all is the same canvas of ocean water.*

Now a voice took up the theme turning the soliloquy into a dialogue. *The expression anonymous mass in their regard is all the more appropriate considering that they are all bereft of a past.* They were deemed to have erased every trace of their personal identity and as such concepts of origin and destination had no reference to them. All that one knew of them was that *they are there*. This circumstance brought to mind the cryptic words of a great sage: I never was nor will I ever be, I AM. Confronted by this anonymous mass of beings all that imagination could do was to ascribe to them an ephemeral fleeting and uncertain identity which was nothing more than an affirmation that each of them was just 'there'. They emerged out of a palette of forms of such immensity and endlessness that they stretched beyond the horizons of mind and imagination. Thus every effort at individual identification became a futile exercise being devoid of supports of space and time. This meant that the forms were interchangeable, that one could be the other.

What relevance has time and space in their lives? he asked his invisible interlocutor. They experienced time as something that did not unfold, that was devoid of duration and was no agent of change. Through their bodies Eternity has irrupted into the temporal order shattering it into bits and pieces transforming it into objects in a juggler's hands. The juggler's hand is the creator of illusion. It induces the observer into a state of trance in which past, present and future with all their accessories of space lose their bearings, their identity, their significance and their purpose. What one sees are objects that appear and disappear all the while seeming to be always there. The thought made him stand still in awe. He thought of the eons and the eons that, without duration and unfolding, were as an instant dream devoid of substance.

****

Now his thoughts focused on himself. During these fathomless periods of time now appearing as a single time and space less scene of the mind, even his ephemeral self had undergone countless changes. He had been clothed with an endless succession of bodies, each with its peculiar form, susceptibilities, dictates and imperatives. If only he could envisage such a past he would not even recognize himself from the unfathomable palette of forms that would be presented to him for scrutiny. The very same reflection equally applied to the envisageable forms which the immensity and endlessness the words 'future existences' would convey. He could indeed point out at random to any one of those countless forms and say: *that's I*. Those multiple manifestations were just himself existing differently. He was an actor of a staged illusion, or maya. His had to be the emotionless attitude of a traveler who was both desert and mirage.

He felt a flood of light within him illuminating a subject which had proved clueless before. He shouted his joy to Mother Ganga. Mother, he said, I have grasped it at last: the issue of birth and rebirth. I considered my 'self' as being unique, assuming one body after another on my path to Awakening. But suddenly light has dawned on me. The enigma of birth and rebirth is appearing to me differently. Now I seem to understand. Mother Ganga's face seemed to light up. Her voice was affectionate and encouraging.

Tell me, mother was saying, *what is your new perspective of the matter?* Mother, I am now convinced that the 'self' of the endless multitude of beings is one and the same. It appears differentiated and individualized in each separate body, but it is the same in all. Mother, the palette of forms incorporating my self since the beginning of my journey towards Enlightenment is the palette of anyone and everyone. That means that I could be each and everyone: even more, it means that I am each and everyone but journeying in a different body. *I understand you*, Mother said. *You are born and reborn in the other and through the other. Now you know what it is to be born and reborn. You merge with and identify yourself with each and every one on the stage of life. You can assume each and every one of those bodies and make them your vehicle on your journey towards Self discovery.*

Comprehension had finally dawned in him that the principal obstacle to his awakening into Divine Awareness was his attachment to his individual self. But here too lay a trap. The death of such a self attached person nevertheless put an end to that self plunging it into the ocean of anonymity and oblivion. What his rebirth would bring about is another self consciousness. *You are right*, Mother Ganga said delving into his mind. *He who tries to save his self will lose it. Once you realize that there is nothing individual about your self, that it is the one and the many at the same time, its uniqueness disappears, and with it your attachment to it. Then only will you realize that you lose nothing in abandoning it. Then only will you realize that awakening into the ONE your Consciousness, become ONE and the Soul of All, will illuminate and enlighten the ocean of anonymity and oblivion in one Infinite, Eternal, and Immortal field of all encompassing, uninterrupted and simultaneous vision.*

****

Life therefore was a continuous revelation to one and the other of their previous births and successive births all occurring before their very eyes and within their own experience. He understood that self and identity were not to be appropriated by one body and one mind at one time in one space. The one and the all were finally all in one and one in all. He thought of the hand of the juggler throwing up identical balls with the consequent annulment of 'a before' and 'an after' for each and every one of them. Indeed each could have been the other with no shade of difference between them at each and every point of time and in each and every place. That each ball attributed to itself a separate identity or individual qualities would not change anything of the picture in the observer's mind. It was what his mind thought that mattered. To the Divine juggler who was both performer and observer each and all were one and the same. Everything would keep appearing and disappearing while seeming to be always there.

Now his mind wandered back to the *Mahabharatha*: just as the *Mahabharatha*, so too his life. It is not contained in a text. The story of his life is there to be picked up and found, salvaged as anonymous treasure from the ocean of story. '*As anonymous treasure from the ocean of story*' he said and repeated over and over again to himself. His life in the ocean of story was an anonymous one. It was he who had identified it with a name, individuality and personality, all contained in a feeling that had seeped into his body and mind and of which they were totally saturated. That feeling was the result of a particular time, a particular place and particular circumstances. Indeed it was the creature of circumstances. Had that story been salvaged at other times, in other places and in other circumstances still that all pervasive and unshakeable feeling would nevertheless not have been any other. Should he only divest himself of that feeling, then he would sink back into that ocean of story and be the anonymous one with all. That was indeed his goal as a renunciate.

****

Once in the dream world he had the anguishing feeling of being separated from his body and not being able to identify it. He knew he was on a seat on that merry go round with no traceable beginning and no predictable end, but which of those bodies doing the rounds was his? How could he identify himself in his most recent physical form? He could be someone in the seats that followed him or in the seats that preceded him. The anguish he was suffering was excruciating. He was separated from himself. He knew that the him he was searching was in the crowd, in the merry ground that was turning round and round. He left his seat and went from the one to the other asking: *are you me*? They gazed at him in wonderment. Some were even amused. Some even asked *what... are you mad or something*? He protested, pleaded and entreated but all to no avail. He knew he was somewhere out there among the others but the search was futile. He was shivering and in the throes of a great fear. He realized that finding himself would be his greatest joy while losing himself would be his greatest anguish.

Then an immense ray of light illumined his understanding. It was he who was riding in every single seat of the merry go round. A sense of relief descended on him. Realization dawned on him that his self, the self of each and every other were all ONE. His self was that of each and everyone and of all, but he experienced only the illusory, ephemeral and transitory one that was unfolding in his individual conscience.

That night awake late into the night before the Ganges he had an uncanny feeling. He felt a light streaming into what appeared as a prism. Now as he watched stupefied, the prism was revealing itself as time and space. The light that had infiltrated into the prism manifesting itself as the Supreme Self had burst into countless selfs that were merging with the bodies molded in the prism by the two hands of time and space. It was the ONE self that appeared as the many over which time and space had thrown the veil of forgetfulness. And then, as if providing an answer to his perplexed mind, he felt his body dissolving transforming him into another and yet another of the infinite number of bodies the prism was generating. With each and every metamorphosis he was experiencing himself as himself but another than what he had been before.

He realized that it was not his sense of 'self' that was in issue but who that self was. What that experience was revealing to him was that the 'who' he is, and was, and will be was finally of no importance and had no significance. It was nothing other than a colouring or clothing the self was assuming in time and space. His task was to divest himself of that colouring and understand the nature of the self within the prism revealing itself as the infinite multitude but which was nothing else than the UNIQUE, the one and only ONE that burst into Consciousness as I AM.

Chapter 12

Temples and Statues

Much as tried to make every passing day fruitful through reflection and contemplation, he did not always succeed in his endeavours. Some days proved to be barren from both points of view. Nevertheless he continued to pace the banks of the Ganges even though that exercise took on the form of a restless, even listless wandering.

He still grappled with the thought of a change of activity in an endeavour to fill the time at his disposal. It was not time that was wanting. The question was how best to spend it? Finally he hit upon the answer. He lived in a country that was pulsating with the heartbeat of the divine. The entire country was dotted with samadhis commemorating saints who achieved total union with the Eternal and the Immortal. The entire country was a site for *Yatras.* He had decided to become a full time actor of his own drama of life. He would walk into the Himalayas, to *Gangotri*, *Badrinath*, *Kedernath* and *Yamunotri*, four to five thousand meters high up, in the regions of the glaciers; of life and death. It was there, in the regions of the rock hard ice covered mountain peaks, of life and death, that one sensed more than anywhere else the throb of the divine.

The Himalayan ranges are possessed by the divine. The entire region looked like a cradle in which divinity had been lulled to sleep. As if to prove its life giving power, it is here that the Himalayan range releases the waters of the Ganges. The river did not look like a river, rather as an energy released from benevolent divine hands, rushing to succour humanity, full of renewed ardour and intent. The next best to pilgrimages to the Himalayan mountains was to live by the Ganges, the gift of the gods to humanity. The miraculous waters personified the divine presence among human beings. That presence was of such an immensity it seemed beyond the reach of his mind. How many gods must I worship and how many *dharshans* must I experience before uniting in ecstatic bliss with the Divinity? he wondered.

****

In the quest of an answer, his mind was now wandering in the innumerable temples that lay scattered over the land of the gods. In each niche of a temple was a statue, many of them *avatars* of the same god. Then as he stood before one niche his mind began to lose its bearings. He was raking his brain in an effort to find out who that god was. Then like a bolt from the blues the thought that seemed to come from a distance of eons approached him at the speed of light and burst into his awareness. *That is I...that is I* he repeated. As he watched enthralled he heard a temple guide explaining to his group of devotees the significance of the statue. This is the god Ganga baba, he was saying. He lived in an unknown period of our history. *No* he shouted, *that is I, I am still alive and before you, here and now.* But no one heard him; no one even appeared to see him. *An unknown period of our history*, he kept muttering to himself. The phrase sounded the same as *countless eons ago* or that which introduced fairy tales, *once upon a time.* His voice within was now speaking to him: *unfathomable are the ways of imagination. That is why time and space can never be unmasked and shown to be a void. The ways of imagination always lead to a when and where, to some place and some time. Imagination, the inexhaustive time and space bank is the filler of the void whatever it be.*

All this while the guide was continuing his narrative. The statue is only a representation. It has no life. The god comes alive only when devotes call out to him during a ritual of worship. Then the statue becomes animated with the presence of the god. He is ready for the *dharshan. Where are these gods when not present in their effigies*, someone asked. They are eons away, the guide was saying, but what are eons but un instant in the field of imagination. *Tell us the story of the god Ganga baba*, a devotee requested. The guide paused as if to recollect. Ganga baba held his breath in expectancy. Then the guide launched into his narrative.

The story of god Ganga baba, like the stories of all gods is one salvaged out of the ocean of story, the repository of myths. They had been drawn out of that ocean which is the mirror of the divine, by the human mind. Like all gods, the presence of Ganga baba is itself not confined to his niche in this temple. *We have made him traverse the length and breath, the heights and the depths in dream and awakened states or whatever other subtle artfulness our imagination is capable of. As with all gods, we made him cover the vast expanses of the land of the gods on foot, before settling him in his final resting place.* This narrative upset him and made him distraught. You made me traverse nothing, he shouted. Your imagination had nothing to do with my life. I am not someone of your past. I am here before you in flesh and blood.

In the midst of his mental turbulence the guide continued undeterred. *He spent most of his life on the lowermost step of the ghat by the sacred river in Rishikesh.* And now the humans undertake the same journeys, in his footsteps and those of their other gods, crossing the waterways of the *tirthas*, the wide expanses of the *ksehtras* before entering their abodes, the *dhams*, wherever they be, in the plains, at the confluences of rivers, in the foothills and in the heights of mountains, in the midst of glaciers. And then his amazement went out of bounds when the guide capped his narrative with his final statement. *Ganga baba's shakthi was maya and the fruit of that union was Neelkanth.*

Then a woman's voice arose from the group. *Tell us about maya. How did she relate with the god*? Maya is the power emanating from the ONE that sets the world up and launches it in the quest of God. *Shakthi* is the love that inhabits the god and sustains him in his endeavour to reveal God to his devotees. In the case of god Ganga baba *Maya* was a love story of his awakened state that reappeared in his dream state, and took flesh and form once again in his awakened state. Her only aim was to live in the dharshan of her god and to offer him the fruit of their love, *Neelkanth.*

But how could he have know that? he asked. *Be a little more discerning*, his voice told him. *There is nothing new in anything he says. Awakened state and dream state form the container and content of every life. There is nothing in your life that was not lived and experienced by someone, some where at some time. For the person with a linear concept of life and belief in a single lifetime, what he does and what happens to him is unique. But for a person with a cyclic notion of life, and belief in incalculable lifetimes stretching over inimaginable expanses of time and space, what he does and what happens to him have been done and have happened over inconceivable periods of time and space.*

What you are witnessing is you narrating your life story. You appear in a state of complete disbelief. Why not take a closer look at the guide? He made his way through the throng which seemed totally unaware of his presence and approached the guide. What he saw left him stunned. He felt the temple turning circles around him and held on to his neighbours for support. It was he himself the guide. Then he heard his voice say: *do not forget that countless aeons have interposed themselves between you and this event which is unfolding. With the passage of those countless eons, when time gets dissected into unknown periods you will become the stuff of imagination. And what is more strange, these countless eons and unknown periods will be evoked and overlap in a flash, in no time, just as you are experiencing here and now. The you that were, that are, and that will be are in you and around you at one and the same time while impersonating every single attribute of time and space.*

He listened dumb founded as the narrative had unfolded and reached its end. He joined the group and continued with the tour listening to the erudite guide. *What exactly is dharshan*? a devotee demanded to know. *Dharshan* is the pinnacle act of worship. It means standing in the presence of the deity and looking at him directly eye to eye. *Dharshan* is seeing the deity and being seen by him. It was visual communication between god and man.

Chapter 13

Gods

He spent his time gazing at the Ganges. For him the Himalayan peaks and the waters of the Ganges were one: the peaks represented the immutable and immovable God while the waters were his mutable and movable presence. The peaks represented god as one, immortal and eternal whereas the waters showed his infinite reflections in their mortal nature subject to ever recurring life and death. He had travelled to *Haridwar* and witnessed the extraordinary celebration that was the *Khumb Mela*. The celebrations had culminated by the god men reveling in the waters of the Ganges. That night seated in his habitual place on the ghat, he felt the presence of the waters as Mother Ganga and discussed many issues with her, mainly about gods, about the Inscrutable ONE and about myths.

Gods, Mother Ganga said will unite in their persons all the states of the human mind, the awakened, the semi awake and dreaming states. They will represent time and space in their most disparate, chaotic and inimaginable forms. They are symbols of the countless passages between life and death which is the field of imagination. They espouse all that mind, feelings, emotions and imagination can conjure. As such they can only find expression in myths. Only myths can furnish the framework and field for such an outflow of creative energy that provide glimpses into the depthless and the unfathomable nature of God. To glimpse this Eternal Truth that is God, one story is not enough: they have to stretch out into infinity. Even infinite myths cannot contain the infinite eternal truth. Humans with their two eyes only see minute aspects of it. The multiplication of stories or myths is the endeavour to glimpse a little more of the inexhaustible nature of the ONE. It is to this end that gods are endowed with countless eyes attributing to them the capacity of greater knowledge of the Truth that is God. That is the reasons why gods are worshipped.

****

But why the thousands of gods? his enquiring mind insisted. How can the eye of the mind capture infinity in a few effigies? It cannot. That is why there are thousands of gods. They are seen as the medium through which Infinity can be glimpsed albeit in little doses. They are endowed with countless physical attributes such as numerous arms, legs, heads, bodies and especially eyes. This is in the hope that they would experience more of the unique Godhead and thereby transmit more of the inconceivable and ineffable divine nature to their devotees through their dharshan. The recompense for all human endeavour is the *dharshan*, glimpsing even for a brief ephemeral instant the One, Infinite and Eternal in whatever manner he deigned to appear through the eyes of the god.

He realized that his life was a divine drama, the drama of God walking the earth in countless forms, human and other, on his way to Himself. His ears rang with the words of a song he often heard in a way side kiosk: *what if God was one of us, just a slob like one of us, just a stranger in a bus trying to find his way home, going to heaven all alone.*

The thought of God walking the earth now received an added impetus in his thoughts. A smile lit up his face when it dawned on him that the song was not at all out of focus. There was much truth in it. Could not God be regarded as lost in any one of us? he thought. If so, our way, the way of each and every one attempting to retrace his steps back home, would be that of God Himself. The thought that God could be lost within him, relieved him of his sense of loneliness. The steps he took in the direction of what he thought was home, would be those of God himself.

He now found a sense of exultation and joy. That joy arose from the conviction that he was finding his way home, that God within him was going home with him; that they were doing the journey back, together. He felt like the driver of a vehicle lost in a fog with a passenger trying to head towards the same destination, but who was as lost as he himself was. They would console each other, encourage each other, support each other, bear with each other, sharing the difficulties that were the lot of lost men. His attitude towards others sharing the same destiny could not be anything else but sympathy, compassion, love and tolerance.

This mysterious presence gave him a new lease of life. The conviction grew within him that he would never become lost on is way home. Should he be unable to continue at the wheel his passenger would take over from him and the journey would continue just with their roles inversed, and as illustrated in the Bhagavad Gita. The stranger would guide the vehicle while he would be lying behind. All this was new to him. It was even exhilarating. Principally however what mattered was that he was not alone. Even more, he would never be alone. If not in the driving seat, he would be a passenger being driven home, by a driver who was God himself.

His mind went back to a similar situation where the driver was God and the passenger of the chariot he was driving, was a warrior going to battle. He remembered their conversations which found written expression in one of the greatest classics of Indian spiritual literature: the Bhagavad Gita. Yet his case was different. His passenger was invisible. The conversation would not be through the medium of sound. The sound between them could only be the sound of silence. The more silent he became the more the passenger's voice would resonate within him. His life now took a different turn. He sought ever more to isolate himself. He sought to still his thoughts. He sought to escape from the clutches of their confluents, the senses.

He had to rein in the flow of events within him, bringing them to a stand still. That stillness deactivated the flow of his sense data and unplugged his senses. It was the only way to increase his powers of awareness and consciousness. That awareness would be the one eye through which one and the other would ultimately know each other, not as one and the other but as one seer with nothing in front obstructing their view.

It was a journey on a path without landmarks, where footsteps left no traces, where eons were as the blink of an eyelid. The only truth was the ONE: *Rama nama satya hai.* There was indeed no one, no thing, and no where wherein god did not dwell, offering himself for the dharshan. Only the eye of the beholder had to be attuned to his presence. The *dharshan* however was only an apprenticeship. The finality of life was not seeing God eye to eye but seeing through the same eye and abiding in Him as the One, Immortal and Eternally Self.

The driver of the transient vehicle and the traveler would finally be revealed as one and the same. It would be a shattering discovery. It was he the very stranger that he bore along. Now he had for once glimpsed the truth of his real home which was identical with his real SELF. With the dawn of Divine Awareness realization would finally dawn that there never ever had been a journey, no one who traveled, no path to travel on, and no vehicle to travel in.

Chapter 14

An Encounter With Shiva

One night after an exhaustive day of walking deeply engrossed in a meditative mood and seated by the Ganges, he fell asleep. Then after an incalculable moment of time he felt himself in unfamiliar surroundings. He was seated by a great river which flowed past with a drowning noise. He looked around but could not identify any object in the range of his visibility. *Where am I?* he asked. What he witnessed next put him in a state of trance, so unbelievable and amazing it was. The waters suddenly swirled at incredible speed and seemed to vapourize. He was reminded of the genie squeezing himself out of the lamp in the story of Aladdin. The waters were metamorphosing into a form, a well built, attractive form of young man. He was attired similarly as he himself was, being draped in a loose yellow robe. His hair resembled a lion's mane but was well kept and represented leonine strength. *Do you recognize me*? The young man was asking him. No, tell me who are you? He replied. *I am the god of Time* the answer came back. You emerged from the waters. How was that? he asked. *What else can better represent Time than the waters*, was the reply. Why have you appeared before me, he asked again. *Because I am your guru*, the apparition answered. *I see you are engaged in a mighty tussle to ferret out the secrets of time*. He looked into the penetrative eyes of the young man. Yes, he replied, that is true. The young man assented. *I have come to answer your questions*, he said. *I came to tell you not to search for time in the present or the future. Time is embodied in THE PAST*.

The calm and quiet nature of the handsome young man emboldened him. What do you mean THE PAST? The apparition laughed. *It means just what it means* he replied humourously. *I am the past of all, whether they be persons or things, and that includes you*. That answer made him reflect. But why only you? Where are my present and my future? he finally ventured to inquire. *There aren't any such. There is only me* The youth was saying. Only you? But isn't it common knowledge that time is composed of past, present and future? The young man smiled. *That is true*, he finally said, *but that is a misconception.*

The composure of the young man clearly indicated that he knew what he was saying. *You look bewildered*, the apparition said consolingly. *The guru does not replace the mind of his adept. I have only sown a seed of wisdom in your mind. It is up to you to nurture it and watch it grow. It will change your life. Now I must go.* he said. No, wait a moment longer, I implore you. I have a few more questions for you. Tell me this. You say you are my past. But I would have conceived the past as bent with age with a hoary and unkept look. On the contrary you are so young, so well built, so beautiful... The youth laughed a loud disarming laugh. *Didn't I tell you that I contain within as well what you consider to be your present and your future*? He laughed again as if struck by the amusing side of his own response.

His mind went to the statue of *Shiva* straddling the Ganges. His right had held the trident. As his eyes fixed themselves on the statue he was invaded by scenes of the Ganga Arti and heard himself intoning the mantra. *Triumbakam Yajamahe Sugandhim Pushtivardhanam Urvar Ukamiva Bandhanan Mrityro Mukshiya Mamritat.* Shiva of the three eyes. Shiva holding he trident, the threefold illusions of time, himself remained distant from it, lost in his own wonderment, contemplating himself as the source of the eternal regeneration of the world.

Then as the scene changed he saw hundreds of flower offerings lit by camphor candles floating down the sacred river to the accompaniment of *om jai gange mata*. He saw the waters as a reflection of the sky illuminated by myriad dazzling stars forming a halo around the Lord of life and death sitting upright and still, lost in the ecstatic contemplation of his divine nature.

****

He came out of his reverie only on hearing the question: *Anything else*? The youthful apparition had by now put on what seemed to be a mischievous look. Tell me, he asked, how can the past be the embodiment of the present and the future? *I will tell you* was the confident answer. *Did you see how the whirling of the waters produced my form?* His interlocutor was looking at him with deep intent. *So is it with all. Everything there is and happens emerges out of a state of flux, a flux of such bewildering speed beyond the capacity of the mind to grasp.* The dreamer seemed perplexed. Do you mean that everything that I see before me is some sort of reproduction of what has flowed past? *That is it*, said the God *that is exactly it. It is the same for the present as well as for the future. The one appears before your eyes, the other in your mind.* He was thrilled by what he was hearing. I never thought it that way, he admitted. So the past is the ground of the present?

His mind began to collect the pieces of the puzzle together. The past is timeless, spaceless, bereft of stability, continuity, logic and reason. The past is my world. I make it to be what I want it to be, and what I make it to be makes me to be what I think I am. What I construe as my past is a multitude of vague impressions like squashed colours on a blotting paper presenting themselves in one single heap for me to pick and chose as building blocks not only of the past itself, but also of the present and the future. The dictates and imperatives according to which I act in making my construction weigh heavily on my mind for evaluating my past as well as my present and future.

So the assumption of a here and now is misplaced too? He enquired. *The idea of here and now is itself a device originating from our need for a sense of fixity and permanence, the sense of feeling rooted somewhere. It is as futile an attempt as trying to build castles with the sands of quicksands on quicksands. But aren't we straying from the matter under consideration? Shall we leave this discussion of the here and the now for another meeting?* The thought of another meeting filled him with joy. Oh yes, with pleasure, he said.

The young man was now looking straight into his eyes. *We were on the theme of the past* he said. *Listen, consider the past, the most distant past, the past at the moment of the unfolding of time. How do you designate such a past?* He was now attuned to that line of reasoning. So he ventured an answer. The beginning, he said. *You are absolutely right*, the youth responded. *Now what is a beginning if not the present?* He repeated what he heard: what is the beginning if not the present, simultaneously recalling what the poet has said: in my end is my beginning. The youth appeared to have read his thought because he said: *That is right,* All *time is finally one. The commencement is at the utmost end of the past and at the furthermost end of the future. Thus when the past and the future have been exhausted, only then will the commencement be all that is. Then only will there be an eternal, everlasting present, an eternal, everlasting NOW.* Tell me, he asked again. What is time? Where is it? The answer was immediate. *That eternal unending, ineluctable and relentless whirl of matter, that is time. As for your second question, the answer is seated in front of you. That eternal unending, ineluctable and relentless whirl of matter that is undifferentiated time, is ME.*

****

At that very moment, on hearing the God's last utterance his eyes were opened and he was overcome by awe and reverence. You are *Shiva*, the Lord of whirling time, and the Lord of the dance. Moments passed by as he struggled out of the throes of his emotions. When he finally did so, he asked a question that had been bothering him since always. Lord, I have heard it been said that you are a myth, that you are not historical? The Lord laughed. *What is myth and what is history but creations of the mind. There is nothing outside the pale of human memory and imagination. They have the same source, the human mind. If they are creations of the mind, it is because the mind has need of them both for life.* The questioner persisted with his question, yes Lord, but what is the more important of the two? The Lord replied: *neither the one nor the other only the truth they connote, only truth is real and not their packaging call it myth or history.*

He recalled how Hindu gods were portrayed as myths. He remembered how religions said to be based on 'history' considered themselves superior to those considered as being based on myths. He recalled how as a young man he had asked a sadhu for his opinion on the subject of history and myth. The reply engraved in his memory was the very same as that he had just heard. The sadhu had said, *neither the one nor the other is important, only the truth they evoke.*

That answer had brought to his mind his experiences at the cremation *ghats* where bodies were taken along to cries of: *Rama nama satya hai* – only God is truth. It was only the truth that mattered for only the truth was real and not the packaging said to contain it. He then felt the dawn approach and that the interview was running to a close. He had time for just one more question. Lord, he finally ventured to ask, how would I know that you are real? The apparition seemed bemused. *Do I seem real to you?* he asked. Of course you do, he replied. But soon I will become awake and you will be gone. The Lord appeared unperturbed by the question. He asked: *what do you mean by 'soon I will be awake'?* As no answer was forthcoming he continued. *Are you sure that your 'awakened state' is not a continuation of your dream?* Tell me he asked. *The things you see, hear, touch, taste, feel and other experiences, can you hold on to them as you thought they were?* Still there was no answer. So he went on. *They all recede continuously and ineluctably into the past, into undifferentiated whirling matter to which memory and imagination try to give a semblance of form, and which your mind accepts in whatever be their condition. The dream state is a much larger and unrestricted field whereas the awakened state is a very limited one. Yet they both emerge and manifest themselves from the same source, which is the past. Each is real for the duration of its experience. One is more akin to myth while the other is more the parent of history. Both the dream state and the awakened state are doors of access to paths that unveil the truth, the reality of life to those dedicated to that search.*

The discourse he was listening to was deep and profound. Lord, he said from what you say would it not be safe to state that it is memory and imagination that bring time into being? The reply was immediate. *Indeed it is memory and imagination that revive the illusion of time. What is real cannot be divested of its reality and made into the unreal. If space and time which were seen as factors that separated, identified, individualized especially by placing events in a chronological order could suddenly only be a hazy blotch in the mind, losing all the attributes we endowed them with, they could not be real. Be it myth, be it history they are creatures of memory and imagination, dependant on their ability to revive the illusion of time.*

Chapter 15

Dreams and Myths

What had caused the turmoil in his thought processes were his dreams. His dreams had been his teachers. Dreams had no past, no present and no future. They were all simulations. He saw them as unfolding but they were susceptible to change with no constant measure either of time or space acting as controls. They appeared as occurring in time but in a time devoid of its role as a measure. It was a time and space framework which remained unidentifiable and chaotic. It was a caricature of time and space. Furthermore when he woke up they were all gone. He could not place them together on a time scale. They were all creatures of a make believe world.

And then he realized progressively that what he considered to be real life had much in common with dreams. While the former occurred behind closed eyes the latter took place before open eyes. What was said to characterize events occurring before open eyes or in the so called 'real' world was their continuity and stability. They were said to be fixable in chronological order. But once they receded to the past, which was immediately after their occurrence, they became a 'buffet' service, for all and sundry to take and use and digest in their own manner. Then the confusions arose. What was seemingly solid and unchangeable suddenly became fluid and mutable. Everything was of the stuff of which dreams are made.

What was most striking about dreaming behind closed eyes and dreaming with open eyes was that as long as both lasted they were seen as being real. When the real became less real or simply irreal and the solid became fluid, time and space measurements became superfluous. In fact the notions of time and space themselves became questionable and doubtful. Everything had a question mark after them. The assessments of truth or untruth, or certainty or uncertainty became the free domain of each individual mind. That meant that reality became subjective. It became a reality that was ideal content for myths. In the dream state behind closed eyes memory and imagination became jugglers dabbling with images and places at will, putting time, space and chronology into derision and yet posing as truth and instilling their content and message in the mind of the dreamer. That was also the function of myths.

****

While his mind was working feverishly trying to tie up his threads of thoughts together, he heard anew what the apparition had said about the relative importance of myth and history: *neither the one nor the other only the truth they connote, only truth is real and not their packaging call it myth or history*. The Lord then said: think of all on the lines I indicated to you, and I will be there to answer you. *No No* he shouted, Lord wait. *Tell me, please tell me, what is maya*? What he then heard was a peal of laughter, youthful, vibrant and supremely joyous. What is maya...what is maya...the Ganges seemed to echo, and then he heard the voice. Maya is going on and on, with an "I" in the middle – but that I is empty and contains nothing. Maya is taking what is transient as permanent; and what is suffering as happiness. It is the state of bewitchment that takes mirage for reality. Yet paradoxically its source is God. It is as if God is putting Himself to the test. It is a test that God Himself appears to shun. Do you recall how the Deathless ONE entered the realm of maya, subjecting Himself to death and sweated beads of blood when directly faced with it. He even cried out: if it be possible, let this cup pass away from me! *Lord*, he said, *I am in a state of bewilderment. How does God cause Maya*?

Listen, let me explain. Bursting out of the sheer exclusivity of Eternity and Immortality God generates within himself the quasi divine tensile strength of Maya which stretches and strains to create its temporal and spatial realm of illusion. The tugging and pulling is of such power that the final yet only apparent release sends Maya whirling, twirling, reeling, gyrating, spiraling and revolving in an incredible spin that surpasses all understanding. The separation will be tinged with joy and sadness much akin to the convulsions taking place at birth, this time at the birth of illusion in the womb of Divine Awareness. Though finally achieving apparent separation the power imparted to the illusory other that is Maya is of such magnitude that it will keep on whirling, twirling, reeling, gyrating and revolving in an infinite display of a fake reality, that of illusory eternity and immortality.

Lord, he blurted, *your description is stupefying. Considering the stranglehold maya has on the mind, is there an escape from it*? The Lord answered: this awesome histrionics and theatrics of visible fixity in the throes of inconceivable change and mutability is only one side of the apparent reality. On the other side of that veil of illusion endlessly unfolding is the even more ecstatic dance of the Lord of life and death, Shiva Nataraja undoing what maya does, revealing the nature of the mirage and calling the mind to sanity. He replied meekly: *I heard Lord.* Then the Lord said: *now watch.*

****

And now the metamorphosis took place in the inverse order. Once again the whirling sound seem to fill the air as the young man swirled at lightening speed and in a blinding light. And so the Lord Shiva Nataraja danced: he danced frenetically swirling at hypnotic speeds. His face changed assuming all traits, his body changed assuming all forms imaginable and unimaginable, his colour changed beyond those of the spectrum. He became the temple of infinity and of infinite time and space. The primordial void and emptiness were manifesting their inconceivable and ineffable potentialities. The opposites merged, distances were annulled the veil of time, of maya, was cast asunder.

And the Lord *Shiva* danced, like sal trees gushing free drunk with the wine of liberty. He danced in gay abandon. He danced as one intoxicated, in a trance, to sounding drum and tinkling cymbal. He danced himself to sheer inconscience in exuberant nudity, pivoting from one foot to the other, his arms flaying the air, reaching the four corners of the cosmos. As he danced he generated desire as his own counterpart, the reflection of his own power, *Shakthi*. Now the one become the other, they danced in tandem, in unison, exulting in ecstatic union of the one with the other. They danced on the stage of their consciousness in sheer bliss, in unbounded joy exulting in their nudity. Their dance was both physical and spiritual, creating the ego and then destroying it, in the blazing flames of their own fiery desire.

Just as *Maya* was seemingly born out of the womb of the Eternal and Immortal, so also was the cosmos being born out of the lightening gyrations of the dancing *Shiva*. The fire generated by the revolutions of the dancing God turned into vapour, the vapour into water, the water into earth and out of these primordial elements arose the incalculable forms themselves assuming illusory fixity while gyrating at the speed of the same spin as its source. The entire cosmos with its infinity of forms would remain circumscribed by fire which in the end would engulf each and every illusion of individuality and separation as in a funeral pyre, reducing them one after the other to ashes. And then the dance would begin anew and the cosmos would rise again out of its own ashes heralding the beginning of a new cycle of existence.

****

Reduced to a state of absolute shock and disbelief he was out of himself shouting out incessantly: *Maya where is your victory, maya where is your sting. Death has lost its sting, the grave its victory. Shiva Nataraja, you are the Lord of the dance. You are the dancer you are the dance. You are the dreamer, you are the dream.* He had once again lost track of time. What he had just witnessed left him dumbfounded. The bewitchment of maya had been lifted, all he saw was the *dharshan* of *Shiva Nataraja*, His body was trembling and swaying as if in the throes of an uncontrollable agitation.

With this realization the mighty waves of emotion that had engulfed him subsided one after the other. He still remained motionless as if trying to find his bearings. Now the gist of the conversation he had just had kept showing up in his mind: *I am your past. As for your present and future, there aren't any, they are misconceptions.* This sentence rang in his mind continuously and did not give him respite. He was now fully awake. By his side the Ganges flowed at its usual rhythm. *What better personified time than the waters?* He visualized the beautiful youth seated cross legged on the waters. Then he thought of the statue of *Shiva* sitting on the Ganges at the Triveni *ghat*. That statue too represented the image of a young man in his prime. Was not *Shiva* ageless? How else can agelessness be represented but by youth and beauty?

He went over to the edge of the waters and looked at his image. What he saw was the form and face of an old man. *It cannot be*, he said. *If I am my past, then I contain my present and my future in me as well. I am Shiva, I am eternal youth, eternal beauty. What I see before me is an illusion, it is maya.* His utterance struck him as being extremely funny. *Shiva, I am Shiva the ageless, the deathless*, he shouted over and over again in bursts of uncontrolled laughter. His shouting caused passers by to stand still, to watch and ponder over the happening. All they saw was an old sadhu, Ganga Baba to some, laughing in a manner hardly imaginable, and dancing for sheer joy. Yet what they saw was maya, but what the old man experienced was out of the reach of their minds. *Oh that is Ganga Baba* some said as they went by, *he is like that, totally unpredictable*. Some found it an occasion to engage in some merriment. So they imitated the dance movements of the old man and stuck their arms and legs in the air while intoning: *Jai Shiva shankara bom bom hare hare*. It lasted a while as the old man kept on dancing uttering the words: *I am Shiva, I am the nataraja, the Lord of youth, the Lord of the dance. I am ageless, I am deathless. I am Shiva*. The moment of ecstasy was over and he was seated at his habitual place on the last step of the *ghat*.

****

The dream had made him pensive. The youthful apparition obsessed his mind and he was desperately trying to draw him once again into his dream world. He knew his culture was founded on myths, and myths were akin to dreams. He thought of the Himalayan glaciers where *Shiva* was enthroned as the Lord of life and death. The glaciers symbolized death, yet it melted and yielded the life giving waters. How often had he travelled from *Rishikesh* into the Himalayan ranges and seen the waters, the life blood of India flowing down into the plains. They came down various Himalayan slopes as independent waterways and united at *sangams*. From then on they continued as one mass that bore the name Ganges.

His dreams were like the waters that streamed down the glaciers in independent beds, while what he saw at daytime appeared as one major river pursuing its course in the plains. Dreams were of a fragmented nature while day life melted them all together into a united front. Day life had all the makings of history and its chronological framework, while dreams had all the making of myths with chronology thrown to the four winds. Myths were closer to the source of truth being the Eternal and Immortal Divine Consciousness just as the independent streams of water streaming down the mountains were closer to their origins, the glaciers. They were closer to the timeless, to the divine. Timelessness was the essence of myths while time was the framework of history. Yet both arose from the same source being memory and imagination.

Myth formation had nothing to do with specific time space frameworks but drew their content from psychological sources such as wishes, emotions, desires, and drives. The content of myths was drawn from a different seed bed than that of history. Considering the fragmented nature of dreams, he saw himself made to appear as the embodiment of fragments of his memory in which parts took possession of his mind and made him live his life differently from what had actually been the case. This was the nature of dreams and led to the answering of unanswerable questions. They were the answers to the questions: what would have been my life if I had followed this or that path? Dreams appeared to make his life seem fuller by taking him along paths he could have trod but never did. Such dream features once again revealed the tinge of remorse and regret that pervaded his sense of the past. The present appeared to be an accessory of the past while the past thus became the simulator of the present and of the future as well.

Chapter 16

An Undying Past

This was also true of his emotional life. The loves of his childhood, adolescence and early youth now seemed to assume greater proportions in his subconscious mind. They appeared to have grown up with him snowballing all the while into a complete love life lived behind the screens of closed eyes. Such loves that had faded away from conscious life now claimed their place through his subconscious mind of the dream world. They now claimed recognition. Dreams seemed to pursue the question how would it have been had we continued our relationship until its full blossoming? Dreams gave more importance to what could have been rather than to what had been. Just like the waters at a sangam, so too the impact of images in the dream world resulted in frothing foamy forms that asked the dreamer to clothe them with the identities that best suited him.

On many occasions he felt obliged to ask himself whether what he saw or felt was happening behind closed eyes or before them. Although he tried to brush away the incident, his confrontation with Maya in the train never receded into the trash bin of his mind. Try as he would to forget, that scene unfolded before him like waves beating against the shore. *Accept the joy your past is offering you on a platter*, Maya had told him. In what form will it come to me? he heard himself asking. It will be the form *that will emerge from the ocean of your sub-conscious, my baba. What matters is joy and its fruit, she had replied*. These words endured within him even deep into the night. The verse of a song he loved to listen to in his youth, now, once again, made itself to be heard. *So deep is the night, no moon tonight, on broken wings my soul hath taken flight, and left a dream*...Indeed every flight of his soul had been a dream. Be it the spontaneous evocation of that meeting or an inner urge, those words kept on humming in his ears. They were invariably accompanied by the vision that had troubled him while in that train, that of a woman and a child. That was the joy that Maya said would emerge from the ocean of his sub-conscious and would be offered to him on a platter. He also heard her say: *It is dreams that take flesh, my baba.* Try as much as he did to suppress it, it had indeed always been his uncontrolled desire that his dreams put on flesh. Maya had done nothing else than read his mind. His desire that that dream take flesh was now seeped with curiosity, the curiosity to see the form or forms his sub-conscious would eventually yield.

Then a sudden light flashed across his consciousness with a message. It said: *There is nothing appearing before open eyes that is not born out of the waters of self desire. The origin of the individual self's desire stretches beyond the reaches of the mind, its memory and imagination, into spheres where time and space are obliterated, to seemingly re-emerge in the blink of an eyelid clothed in form. There is nothing appearing before open eyes, the realm of imperiously reigning time and space, that is not molded in the kingdom behind closed eyes where time and space reduced to utter servility are like play things in a juggler's hands. The outside world if asked about its origin would invariably reply: I remember being born in a dream world; I remember emerging out of a dream world.*

While pondering over these issues his mind dwelt on a curious encounter that occurred during one of his meditative walks along the sacred river on the outskirts of the *Luxman Jhula* bridge. He felt he was being followed. He had noticed a woman carrying a child behind him at a certain distance who slowed down her pace and even stopped the moment he did so. This had been going on since some time but he had not attached any importance to it. However he was now certain that he was the object of her attention. On one occasion he had sat down on a rock and left her no other alternative but to approach and pass him. Their eyes had met for a fleeting moment and that eye contact had left him in a troubled state of mind. The look she had directed at him continued to haunt him.

As he sat still he felt hemmed in from all sides by seated and standing figures while the rock on which he sat began to shake and rattle. He was once again in the train that was carrying him to Haridwar. He saw the face of Maya peering at him and she was speaking to him telling him what he had heard once before and was now hearing again: *The world of open eyes has nothing more to offer you my baba. They can never fill your real and as yet unrealized yearnings embodied in your invisible person. I am your unrealized dream my baba. It is not I who am pursuing you. It is you who are unconsciously calling me up from your formless depths within which I lie. From the depths of your being you are crying out to me my baba. You will not stop doing so until I become flesh and blood.*

Then, proceeding from what seemed to him to be a distant ocean, the figure of a woman carrying a child was being wafted to where he sat over incessantly rolling waves. He watched as the waves came nearer and nearer riding on high tide and bringing their objects along. All this while his heart pounded harder and harder as if vying to emulate the rattling of the train. He was watching stupefied as the waters deposited their human cargo directly in front of him.

Who are you? he asked. At first she did not seem to understand his question. Then an air of bemusement appeared on her face and she answered with a question of her own: *Why baba, my baba, can you not remember*? He wanted to say 'no' but something was holding him back. She was still standing and watching awaiting his reply as he raked his mind for a past that he seemed to remember but which was eluding him. All this while amidst the rattling of the train that continued Maya was saying: *Accept the joy your past is offering you on a platter*. In what form will it come to me? he heard himself asking. *The form that will emerge from the ocean of your subconscious, my baba*, she said. *What matters is joy and its fruit*. Sensing that something that was within his grasp and brought to him over the oceans of existence by the waves of time was now filtering through his fingers he cried out desperately: No, wait, do not go away. *Nothing goes away that does not come back my baba*, came the reply.

Still seated and shaken by his experience, he felt a hand on his shoulder and a concerned voice asking him: *Are you alright? I saw you talking to someone who seemed to be standing right in front of you. I felt you were raking your mind to recall your past. But remember, though tide and tide are said to wait for no man, nothing is once and for all. The word never has no sense, but the word ever does have one. It is a word that seems so abstruse and unfathomable. Yet it has such a simple connotation: it simply means 'now'.* Suddenly the thought struck him that all religions end their prayers with the word 'now' reinforcing it with the expression 'for ever'. Imparting to the simple a needless aura of incomprehensibility and mystery was an art all religions thrived on at the expense of the gullible, he mused.

He decided not to take that particular path for some time hoping that the incident would be forgotten as one of no consequence. Yet the image of the woman and the child continued to disturb him cropping up again and again in his mind. This was especially so because of the resemblance they bore to the woman and child of his dream while in the train from his home to *Haridwar*.

****

With this incident he had unwittingly once again begun to grapple with his past. When he entered into the state of *sannyasi*, it was with the intention of making the present count for his future life. So had he conceived his life from the very beginning. The 'was' was said to influence the 'is', while the 'is' was said to have repercussions on the 'will be'. But his experiences were making him to change his perspectives of things. His present was becoming more and more a field of propitiation for the past. He was realizing that his present was given to him to redeem his past.

It was in this perspective that he was beginning to see the penitentiary practices of his fellow *sadhus*. All the pain they were inflicting on themselves was not to better their future but to redeem their past. It was the past that held the key to whatever other divisions of the time the mind conceived and which were nothing else than mental manipulations. The past was the energy field that lit up the flickering flame called the present that threw its imaginary shadow on a nowhere called the future. The NOW would be nothing other than the total redemption of the past with the complete wiping out of its slate. With the total emptying of the energy field of the past so would the future be erased and what arose from that effacement would be the Eternal and Immortal NOW in its unending pristine beauty, its unending pristine youth, its unending pristine vigour. While all this was occurring in his mind reduced to a state of turmoil, the sun had risen and set. It was now night. He looked at the waters and bowed his head to the ground murmuring: *Om Namah Shivaya*. Soon he fell asleep.

Chapter 17

Dream State and Awakened State

While he slept, his mind attuned to dreams merged in the flow of certain events with which he readily identified himself and experienced as ongoing occurrences. He had arrived at a stage where his dream state and his awakened state merged seamlessly, like a tapestry woven with same thread of consciousness. Getting up with the body was only getting out of one sleep into another, like getting out of one bed into another. All life, he realized was a dream, and dreams are nothing but dreams.

Once recalled from the past, an event appeared as happening in the present. And so he felt himself engaging in a journey, a journey filled with deep nostalgia for all it evoked. He saw himself walking yet again deep into the night but now he was alone. At what seemed a distance of aeons he saw a white dot appear out of the darkness. It seemed to stay immobilized as if inviting him to approach. His eyes now lit up at the vision of the point of light. He continued walking with his slow uncertain step. He did not know how much time had elapsed. He only knew that he was engulfed in the darkness with only that white spot of light indicating the way. From time to time he noticed that the spot was becoming bigger.

Then finally, in what once again seemed aeons, it burst into his view like the pyramid shape of a white mountain peak.'*The Shivling*' he cried out, '*the Shivling*'. *The Lord is my light, the Lord is my light* he repeated over and over again like a religious mantra. He did not feel alone anymore. He felt the benevolent presence of the Lord showing him the way. He was in the midst of a *dharshan*. The vision seemed to last an entire night though the sense of time had escaped him totally. Then out of timelessness time and space burst into his view with the sudden dawn of day. It was as if that initial white point had burst open in a flash of golden hue as the sun emerged over the horizon. The darkness had vanished as if by a single thrust of a white pointed spear.

The only point of identification had been that white dot of light that had expanded to enfold everything within the four horizons in which he stood. He had felt lost in that immensity until that light revealed itself to him. Then suddenly a different feeling of awareness began to take possession of him. That shining white dot of light was itself a sensation and therefore could be no where else but within him. Perhaps his destiny did it lie in merging with that dot and expanding with it to enfold the universe and all in it? The self that he knew and cherished and protected was a lost cause in that immensity. He would have to relinquish it, just let it go. It was only then that the ray of light present within him could emerge, draw him into the vortex of the ocean of light and reveal to him his true and only identity.

The prospect seemed frightful at first because there is nothing of greater worth to a person than the self he knows. He could not barter it for the whole world. Fear it was that held him to the world that was his. But the price he would have to pay for that fear was that of endlessly dying and being reborn, entering again and again on the stage of *Maya* and leaving it on being dragged away each time by *Mara*. It was as if the Lord of life was being held to ransom by his own creation.

He gazed once more at that fear inspiring deathlike whiteness and stillness that was the *Shivling*. Within it lay the hibernating fire of life itself. It was all within him. *Let go, let go of your transient self, merge with your Real Self and be what you really are. Be still and know that you are God.* His head was reverberating with the vibrations of that sound. His decision had been taken. While looking outward and following the nascent light embodied in the dot, it dawned on him that he was really on an inward journey; his mind turned inwards seeking out the spark of light at the end of the dark tunnel of his own mind.

****

The mountains and their triangular peaks bearing the resemblance of sitting and meditating ascetics now loomed all around him. The whiteness they displayed looked at times like a mortuary shroud thrown over a corpse. Yet at other times it was translucent as if radiating an inner life. They were indeed symbols of life and death by their icy coldness on the one hand, and the life giving waters that trickled down their precipitous lower slopes.

The icy cold hand of death seemed omnipresent but within those silent sentinels of immortality embedded as a germ of life within a womb lay a spark of life, a hidden '*amritam*' the nectar of immortality which was the prerogative of God. There could be no rebirth without death and death meant being reduced to ashes, the return of every single atom of one's body to its creditor, mother earth. Mother earth was not a usurer who demanded an ounce more than what it had lent, but it takes back everything it gives. The body is not a gift but a loan. Yet death can be simulated with the body emptying itself of all its accumulations and accretions through the transformation of the mind.

Many ascetics adopted the technique of wearing the body out. Some did it by trudging the length and breadth of India, visiting holy places being temples and places of pilgrimages. Others gave themselves up to severe forms of penances, assuming rigid or contorted bodily positions until their limbs became atrophied and their eyes were blinded. Other subjugated their bodies by depriving them of essentials such as food and water. Still others tortured their bodies in unimaginable ways, rolling their whole length over thousands of kilometers, hanging from iron hooks and sleeping on metal nails. As for him, he sat in the biting cold in imitation of the mountain peaks and assuming their death like stillness and silence. What would one not go through to possess that drop of 'amritam' or the life giving spark of immortality?

****

Finally he reached the tapovanam and sought out a rocky outcrop under which to place his meager belongings and to set up his make shift abode. Then after a long moment of well earned rest he laid a woolen rug outside his tent, sat on it letting his mind take in the surroundings. His eyes skimmed the horizons which now seemed to lie within him. Progressively their presence began to overwhelm him. Not only was time of no concern but he had absolutely no feeling of time to feel concerned about. With its disappearance the feeling of space itself faded away. And then, after what seemed an eternity and of a sudden it began.

Chapter 18

Samadhi

First there was a vibration which was the breath of life that took sound as OM. The awareness was manifesting itself as life. It was moving like the rising sun diffusing light. The light stretched into infinity and with it came the experience of deathlessness. Then came awareness of all dimensions: Length, breadth, hypnotizing heights and abysmal depths. There was no mind to evaluate and assess, only awareness, a living experience of the creator undifferentiated from creation. That awareness was pure exhilaration, beyond thought, beyond words, beyond images, all that was associated with body and mind. That awareness was wind and blew where it willed, it was earth that descended to fathomless depths and rose to dizzy heights. It was flowing as liquid, streaming down the mountains slopes, falling over ravines, precipitating itself through gorges and transforming itself into mighty oceans that heaved from unthinkable depths like awesome coils of a mythical serpent. That awareness was transforming itself into infinite forms, minuscular, small and big, floating in the air, crawling and walking on land and swimming in the waters. Nothing was static; nothing was once and for all. *Behold*, awareness was saying, *I make all things new.*

It was a continuous happening as a deep inhalation that seemed like incalculable aeons, and a deep exhalation which itself too evoked countless aeons. That awareness was one of breath. Indeed *the One breathless within Himself exhaled outward* and from that divine breath rose the cosmos with all its splendours. That awareness was the breath of ecstasy, of bliss of joy. Out of it, like out of an unseen ocean rose a gigantic wave that reverberated with the words: *God will wipe away every tear, there will no more be weeping and death. I am Being, I am knowledge, I am Bliss.*

He finally came to the awareness that everything pertaining to existence, births and rebirths, even notions of immortality and eternity were imagination culled from thoughts, until the *dharshan* replaced both making the seer and the seen into ONE. And when *dharshan* did provide the final answer then yet again the question would arise, whether it was a dream state or an awakened one. The seal of certainty would come only from conviction whatever be the state, dream or awakened, and that made the issue still more a personal one. He felt he was turning around in a merry go round, waiting for conviction to show the exit door out of the labyrinth. The more the *dharshan* appeared real the stronger would be the conviction, and the stronger the conviction the greater the peace of mind it would engender. Conviction was the powerful wind that calmed the turbulent waters of his mind.

The truth of it all was there were no objective yardsticks to gauge the departure point, the progress and arrival line of the conscience towards its complete realization as Divine Awareness. There would only be a personal measure being that of detachment from the illusory self. The more one is detached from one's self the more it relinquishes its hold on the individual conscience. That is effectively the measure of the truth of the dharshan in its definitive form where the eyes too instead of looking into one another merge into the unique eye that is Divine Awareness.

****

He was now seated before the pyramid shaped form of the *Shivling.* As he watched enthralled a dazzling scene was unfolding. Layer after layer of the rock solid ice that clothed the mountain contours seemed to melt yielding the life giving waters. They flowed like blood running through the numerous vein like formations in the earthen basin at the feet of the mountain ranges. But more was to come. As his mind became engulfed in the interior scene the layers that detached themselves from the mountains seemed like as much clothing divesting the body for which they served as covering. What was emerging before his bewildered eyes were the contours of a human form, seated in the same posture as himself. He felt his body undergoing an irresistible transformation. His skin was taking a marble like hue while his physical form was expanding and filling his interior spaces. He felt himself levitating above the flowing waters and his posture became imperious.

And then there emerged vibrations sounding like a mighty wind which grew louder and louder and finally burst on him taking the form of the mantra: *Om Namaya Shivaya.* He heard the voices of myriad devotees acclaiming him with the words: *come down Shiva, come down. Come down singing, come down dancing, bring us the spark of the divine.* The entire Himalayan framework was shaking to its depths as if called out of its deep slumber by the voices of devotees ringing in unison. They were calling out to him to reveal himself as joy, as bliss, as ecstasy through their greatest expression which was the dance, the dance that was the supreme manifestation of his divinity and his overlordship over life and death.

Joy, joy, joy, the word was echoing in the mountains. Joy, joy, joy, the word was echoing in the plains. The wind wafted the word charged with every sentiment and emotion to the extreme horizons. The waters flowed in ecstatic joy. The earth displayed every hue and colour at the sound of the magic word. They were all not just witnesses but bearers of the revelation of the Eternal, Immortal Self and its dharshan. How could they exist but in the throes of ecstatic joy and bliss? Joy was streaming down the glaciers like a mighty river that had burst its banks. It was a joy that nothing could contain, not even the ice-clad mountain peaks of the mighty Himalayas. The waters of joy would now flow out over every obstacle, over ravines and gorges, over great falls and inundate the earth with the message: *We are the Self, the Great, the Immortal, the Eternal.* Joy was now revealing itself as enjoyment, unbridled, frenetic enjoyment.

****

The mighty Himalayan range now rumbled as God assumed his role of actor of the divine drama that was unfolding within every human mind and heart. The cosmos had become Shiva's theater and the dance was about to commence. The stage was now set for him to emerge. And when he did he felt his arms extended holding aloft the heavenly vault while his feet tapped the four corners of the earth to the rhythm of the drum he held in one hand and was beating with his fingers. His mystic loneliness was being overcome in the rapture of primordial ecstasy. His movements were revealing his immense delight to be, while his vision skimmed across unending horizons. *Shiva nataraja, shiva nataraja, Lord of the dance, Lord of creation* he heard the universe rumbling in homage. All the while the mighty Ganga flowed silently under him. *Am I dreaming* he wondered? *Is this a dream? No it could not be, it was so real...so real.* '*I am 'Shiva'* he cried out and his voice filled the spaces around him. *I am Shiva Nataraja the Lord of the dance, the Lord of creation.*

His body was now on fire. He was the waters, he was the fire, he was the earth, he was the air. He filled all the spaces. He experienced the Earth breathe and come alive. With his movements the universe was taking shape, the sun, the moon, the stars, the galaxies. The fire had now turned into Light. As he whirled and twirled the universe began to move and it was happening. Here was no within and without, no inside, and no outside. He was the ONE and he was the ALL. His face lit up in a smile of silent enjoyment. It was his being that was unfolding that gave everything its form and set everything in place. It was all as he willed it to be. In him was everything and outside him was nothing.

****

How long it all lasted he did not know and did no care to know. It was happening and lasting and enduring beyond the widest stretches of his mind and imagination. He did not want it to end. His body had lost its hold on the mind and is mind was receding out of his consciousness. He had totally dissolved into Awareness. What was being transacted in that boundless hall of Awareness in an atmosphere of total ecstasy and bliss was the act of creation. And then he addressed all creation.

Shiva, I am the Lord of death, but it is a life bringing death. I am the Lord of the dance. My dance is inconceivable to the human mind. It is quicker than the speed of light. It creates the world of *Maya*. My dance makes the world of *maya* look solid and perennial. The rapidity of my dance hides the fact that the nature of the world is flux and mutability. In each individual, my dance creates an energy zone. This energy zone produces a flickering flame which casts its glow over nowhere. You call this ensemble of aspects of my dance, 'time'. The energy zone you call it the 'past': the flickering light it generates, you call it 'present' and the shadow that flickering light throws over nowhere you call it 'future'. The essential element is that non-dimensional energy zone, the past. The past is an approximation of death. Yet the past is not death. It is productive of the present and the future. It is your destiny to merge with me in my dance and escape the world of *maya*. Thus merging with me you will comprehend that the dancer is not maya but Shiva.

It cannot be he heard himself say, *no it cannot be, am I dreaming*? He tried to shake himself out of his state, he pinched himself, he touched the ground on which he was seated. *No it was no dream, and what if it was*, he said to himself, *what if it was, does it matter. If that was a dream then let it be. It that be a dream let me never become awake ever again. If that was a dream I will never cease being in love with night and will never more pay worship to garish day.* He even recalled the words of the poet: *O man, take care! What does deep midnight declare? I was asleep. From a deep dream I woke and swear. The world is deep. Deeper than day had been aware.*

****

Now awareness dawned on him that he was living an illusion. He realized that his body was mind stuff. He realized that the physical form whatever it be and wherever it be, presented itself to his mind only as a sensation. It was sensations that the mind endowed with the primary qualities of hardness, fluidity, length, breadth, height and weight. Such was the construction of reality by the mind. What the mind constructed presented itself to the sensory organs as such. Hardness for instance lived up to the reality it had been endowed with: so too with weight. Every object existed in accordance with the qualities the mind attributed to it. His was a life founded on and formed by *maya*. The experience he was just emerging from had rent that veil of maya asunder and revealed to him reality as it really is.

And then he felt the light dimming and losing its intensity. He felt the flow of the waters subsiding and vanishing from his sight. He felt the horizons shrinking just as was his body. It was happening in the inverse order but still seemingly taking an eternity. He had by now ceased to be the Seer. He felt his body. He felt the cold. He felt the rug under him. Still he refused to open his eyes, he wanted so much that it happen again and again. After what seemed ages he opened his eyes. He saw himself surrounded by reverent onlookers. He was now clothed in garlands, they were prostrating themselves at his feet. He saw food and victuals placed all around him in abundance. He heard the refrain: *Om Namaya Shivaya* addressed to him. He did not want to know how long he had been transported to the beyond. He felt that it had all happened NOW. For the duration of his ineffable experience he had discovered his real identity as Divine Awareness and Divine Awareness is what is.

He did not want to rise up. Now all he wanted was to remember and live in that remembrance. His life could never be the same. How would he react towards the world? He would like many who had experienced such a state take refuge in silent enjoyment of that revelation, continuing to live in the remembrance of that bliss and ecstasy. Then his consciousness dissolved once again, this time from the state of dream to that of a profound dreamless sleep. But just before that a final thought intruded into his dreaming mind: *sleep is simulation of death. Like dreams to sleep, so too in the sleep of death could dreams arise.*

It had all been only a dream. He had covered a thousand miles experiencing it only as the rising and falling of forms within a Consciousness that had overflowed the limits of his individual self. Yet he had never left his moorings; he had never left his dwelling place. He was IT, he was THAT. Before the mountains were born he was; before the earth and the world were formed he was. So he was from eternity to eternity, from the eternal past to the eternal future. A thousand years were merely a yesterday to him, a night watch, like sleep. As the curtain fell on his personal drama he heard a voice like that of the winds say:

even the darkness will not be dark to you;

the night will shine like the day,

for darkness is as light to you.

Chapter 19

Neelkanth

The Ganges became the center and focal point of his life. Much of his time was spent pacing the numerous walks along the banks of the Ganges. When night fell, he spread his clothes on a step of the *ghat* as bedding for the night. When it rained he sought out the shelter of a shop facade. One night fallen into a heavy sleep he was suddenly awoken in the midst of a violent downpour. In a few seconds he was soaked to his very bones and was shivering in the cold. He had not even the time to stand on his feet and contemplate his next move when he felt a plastic covering being held over his head and someone trying to raise him. He leaned heavily on the arm extended to him and pulled himself up. Then he heard that very same voice that time and again erupted from within his memories. It said: *do not worry my Baba, everything is alright*. He noticed he was flanked by two figures, that of a woman and a little boy. He immediately recognized the woman as the one who had followed him in the outskirts of the sacred river. Her voice and presence had an electrifying effect on him, she had addressed him as '*my baba*'.

He was still having difficulties in finding his bearing when he was led away. He was led through an inner lane into a little house. Still drenched he settled down on a rug on the floor while the woman brought him warm clothes. She also placed warm cloth on the ground for him to lie down and sleep. Then she left him. The little boy however remained by his side and assisted him as he rid himself of his drenched clothing and put on the fresh ones. When finally he laid himself down on his new bedding, the little child stayed on and slept by his side.

He spent a restless night trying to fathom the mystery of this womanly presence and her child. Once again the image of his dream took possession of him. His mind was like a boat rocking on turbulent waves. When morning finally dawned the woman brought him a steaming mug of tea and discretely retired from the scene. The little boy however lingered on. When ready to leave, he looked around for his benefactress but noticing that she preferred to stay away, he left the house still accompanied by the little boy, and made his way to the *ghat*. The boy was carrying his new clothes to his habitual abode.

When he finally set himself down and turned around he noticed the presence at a distance of the mother, who was watching them and waiting for her son to come back. At lunch time the little boy brought him his food on a paper plate. Ganga baba did not speak but showed his gratitude as best as he could by a nod of his head or by raising his hand in the gesture of '*shanthi*' meaning peace. The boy now addressed him by the name '*papaji*'. He felt the constant concern of the woman in his regard. She appeared from time to time to see how he was faring, and sometimes gazed at him fixedly in the manner of devotee waiting for the *dharshan* of her god.

****

The boy spent his free time seated at a respectful distance from the *sadhu*. He now had many friends in the neighbourhood. Their mothers who were wont to do shopping in the area found a convenient way of keeping their own little boys in safe custody while they went about their daily chores unhindered. They would leave them on the steps of the ghat where their little friend kept vigil over the aged ascetic. On their return the mothers would gather their children from their place on the *ghat* and then address their homage to the baba. Before leaving they would invariably eat a snack, order a drink and make purchases from the shop next to which Ganga Baba spent his time and where and slept at night.

The shop owner who benefitted by this new situation was conscious of the love that was developing between the old ascetic and the little boy. He had seen the little boy seated by the side of the *sadhu* as the latter sat motionless, his eyes fixed on the Ganga.

No words were spoken but it was obvious that a mysterious current of tenderness passed between the old wanderer and the little boy. On one occasion he had seen a group of quarreling dogs approach the *sadhu*, when the little boy had rushed in between them his hand held aloft in a gesture of protection for the *sadhu*. He had seen he *sadhu* touch the shoulder of the little boy in a reciprocal gesture of thanks. To show his own thankfulness for the extra profits his shop was making, he gave the boy a gift of rupees hundred in full view of the old renunciate. The boy in turn tendered it to the old ascetic who made a gentle gesture of refusal. Then he ran towards his mother and handed the money to her. She took it over to the same shop and after profusely thanking the owner bought a blue coloured school bag for her son who was on the verge of attending school.

With the further passing of time the interest the old man showed towards the little boy grew into paternal concern. He did not know anything about the woman nor the child, or so he thought. But many things worried him. That her face was familiar had struck him since the beginning. Now he even seemed to recognize her voice. What troubled him most were the words '*my baba*' she used in addressing him which revived intimate memories of his dream world. Then there was the way she looked at him with the same mixture of recognition and love. He grappled incessantly with these riddles without being able to fit the pieces of the puzzle together.

****

One day the *sadhu* heard some rustling which he realized was the contact of a woman's clothing against the steps of the *ghat*. Then he saw her prostrating herself before him and heard her voice addressing him. She was thanking him for a gracious act on the part of the shop keeper solely accomplished out of respect for Ganga baba. He had volunteered to get her son into a nearby school and to pay his monthly school fees. He had told her that since the *sadhu's* association with his shop, his business had visibly improved and he ascribed it to the grace of the holy man. With his gesture he was making his offering of thanks to God, he had said.

Then one day, he heard the same rustling of the dress. He saw mother and son prostrating themselves before him. He saw the little boy with his little blue bag dangling behind his back from his neck. It was to be his first day in school. The boy was dressed in a little blue pair of shorts and a little blue shirt to match. The silent *sadhu* was deeply moved. As he touched the boy's head, something mysterious took place. Out of the depths of his memory as if through invisible stirrings, a word burst out and left its print on his mind. It was the word "Neelkanth'.

At school the formalities of enrollment were in progress. What is the boy's name? asked the director. 'Neelkanth' replied the mother. Who is the mother? The director continued. 'I am', was the mother's reply. The father? There was a pause. Before the mother could reply the boy answered, 'Ganga Baba'. The mother pressed him against her side in a gesture which meant: *keep silent*. My husband left us to become a wandering ascetic, she said by way of an explanation. Do you know where he is? was the immediate question. This time before the boy could answer, the mother said: no.

That evening the same gesture as of the morning was performed as the duo returned from the boy's school. This would happen day after day. The old ascetic whose awareness of the time had been drowned in the flow of the Ganges, now had a point of reference for time's passage. It was the presence of Neelkanth, the name by which he identified the boy hardly knowing that that was his real name.

Chapter 20

Living With the Ganges

The space Ganga Baba had chosen for his night's rest was the lowermost step of a *ghat* by the Ganges. He sat there contemplating the waters as it flowed gently by. What was particularly attractive about the Ganges was that it was flowing and that all everyone heard from it and about it was the noise of its flow. People attributed to it all that their thoughts, sentiments, emotions and imagination could muster. The river however did not react in any conceivable manner. It simply flowed by according to its dictates which were those of nature.

He sat on the lowest step of the *ghat* and remained still for long hours. He was trying to catch the mysterious sounds of the river. The gentle flow soothed his mind and acted as a balm to his heart. Watching and listening he felt himself being carried away on the undulating waves to an unknown destination. That destination would be the ocean. No, not the ocean to which the Ganges was heading, but an ocean nevertheless in its endlessness. In its own ocean the Ganges would lose itself. It would cease to be the Ganges. He compared his nature to the incessant flow of the waters. The flowing waters always found their way. They heaved themselves over obstacles and made their way through every barrier the terrain placed before them. So it had to be with him, on his way to his final destination.

He carried with him the image of the Ganges in his meditative walks in the surrounding hills. He considered himself to be a stream that weaved its way over the jagged and protruding rocks and stony descents. The waters asked no questions and advanced no answers. All nature bowed its head to the greatest law that governed the co-existence of the elements, that of gravity. His own nature was ruled by a gravitational pull. All mortal natures gravitated towards sickness, old age and the culmination of life in death. That was uncontestable. The clearest proof of that was his own resolve to renounce to all his worldly possessions, human and material, and prepare in a worthy manner by resigning himself to the inevitable.

Unlike the Ganges, his head was full of questions, and though answers propped up a plenty they had not succeeded in dissipating his doubts. His mind went back yet once more to the Ganges. The river had no question, no answers and no doubts. It simply flowed as dictated by its nature. The Ganges knew its nature. The sounds that emanated from it seemed to him to be those of contentment, the contentment that came in knowing its identity, its origin and its destiny.

Chapter 21

Maya

When sleep finally came it was never total. The night did not fall on him like a heavy curtain on a stage blotting out what transpired on it. With sleep the stage changed as did the setting and the actors. It was never a continuity with what he experienced in his awakened state. He began to note certain common features of which his dreams were constituted. Many of them took him back to his childhood. He recalled the words of the bard: *in my end is my beginning*. The figures that stood before him often lacked clarity. They looked hazy. It was his mind that told him who they were. So it was also with the background which seemed to emerge from a mist. But all that seemed irrelevant. They were all what he thought they were, and nothing less. The imprint of the mind on his world was always the determining factor of its apparent reality and authenticity.

One recurrent figure was the girl, his student, who had once loved him and whose name was Maya. But their paths had separated. Subsequently she had left the State to live elsewhere. He had met her again on a few rare occasions with their contact being confined to a mere exchange of a few words. But she did return to meet him, in his dreams. He had told her of his wish to leave all his earthly concerns behind him and disappear from his society into oblivion. He saw her unhappiness and the tears that streamed down her cheeks. His dream vanished with her parting words: *wherever you are I will find you my Baba. Though the light of the sun hide you from me, the light of the moon will not, for the moon is a woman, the moon is Maya*. He recalled the words of the poet: *wait for me by moonlight, watch for me by moonlight, I will come to you by moonlight though hell should bar the way*. From then on she had appeared to him time and again, the last occasion being on his train journey. But many years had elapsed since he last saw her.

After what seemed a very long lapse she did return to meet him. When she did so, it was with a bulge of her stomach indicating the beginnings of a pregnancy. She told him that she was with child through him. *What was happening*? he asked himself. *Am I dreaming or is this real*? At first a sense of panic struck him, but it subsided. What succeeded was an upsurge of joy at the thought of being a prospective father. No it cannot be, he heard himself utter as he tried all he could to suppress that feeling. It was to him without the least justification.

****

There was one thing that puzzled him. Each time he saw her he had the impression that countless years had elapsed since their last meeting. Furthermore the apparition that presented herself under that name bore only a vague resemblance to the young woman he had first come to know. All these womanly forms were merging with the identity the same name 'Maya' indicated. *How could this be*? he asked himself as his perplexity grew. The name he had identified, but not the form and surely not the circumstances. Yet the woman who appeared before him imposed herself on him as being his student who once was the love of his life.

Whatever that be, reality was what his mind told him that it was. *It is only the name that matters*, his subconscious mind was telling him. *Just look at the numerous statues bearing the name of the same god. Are any two of them alike? Yet you bend in worship before the name. It is the name that tells you that the embodiment is the same.* Was if god had assumed the form of the woman Maya? *If so, I cannot reject her. But how could I know? Only time will tell*, he uttered consolingly, *only time will tell*. Time was indeed the when, the why and the what of all. Time was the avatar of the Godhead. She appeared to sense the doubts that surged in his mind. And then she was speaking as if to lay his doubts to rest. *Baba, do you remember how I once requested an explanation about tantric love? Do you remember how assiduously I took down notes as you spoke. Baba I carry these notes with me as a reminder of our love.* Then she pulled out a paper from her bag and began reading:

****

The mass of flesh and bones known as the "body" is actually one vast field of energy or light. In the ultimate experience, the I and the you relationship breaks down. We both dissolve into the seamless Unity that we have always been. This understanding elevates the body (and thus the entire material world) into the realm of the sublime. Together we become a divine dream. Thus for *Tantra*, the body takes on profound significance: it is an actual "temple of the Divine", a temple where *Shiva* and *Shakthi* meet and merge together in the oneness of physical love.

Our world is that of *Shiva* and *Shakthi* It is only when these two merge through our bodies that we attain that total luminosity or the ocean of pure awareness which is our true nature. It is only then that *maya* the illusion disappears. To overcome *maya*, the I and the you, male and female, must unite. That desire to unite even though sexual in nature is a divine energy. This energy makes man and woman merge together as *Shiva* and *Shakthi*. It draws *Shiva* to *Shakthi* and *Shakthi* to *Shiva* in the one divine temple of love. Though generative and procreative it culminates in ecstasy through orgasmic release. The goal of such a union is beyond sensory pleasure being ecstasy which is the ultimate state of Enlightenment, of Pure Bliss. Such ecstasy results in the burning of the 'self' into ashes just the way it happens to the body on a cremation pyre.

Do you remember my Baba, she was asking him. That is what you told me. You told that to me over and over again and I have retained every word you said. Do you remember the night you and I became *Shiva* and *Shakthi* in the temple of physical love? That night was the most ecstatic night of your life you told me. I could not reply because the ecstatic transport that I experienced left me speechless, Baba. That was my first such experience and it will also be my last. Then the scene receded and was soon enveloped in the mist. As her features were vanishing he faintly caught her last words: *I will come back baba.* Yes indeed he remembered that particular lecture and the notes he had dictated which the dream figure had read out verbatim to his utter consternation and amazement.

****

At first he resented being assailed by dreams because it was like being dragged back to the life he had forsaken. It was as if he was taking back the body which had symbolically been reduced to ashes on the funeral pyre during the ceremony of his initiation to the life of *sannyasi*. Yet he began to long for his dream states. While they lasted they were real. He experienced them as genuine and authentic. He did not even realize that they were dreams. In his mind he was awake while persons and events were unfolding before his eyes.

There were nevertheless differences from the awakened state. The light appeared to him as dim, more like the moonlight as contrasted with the garish light of the day. His attitude towards the moon too was changing. He began to long for night fall and hope the moon would manifest herself. The moon became the only feminine element of his life. She was round, curvaceous, her light was discrete and moderate. There was no semblance of violence about her, she was soft and sweet and appeared timid veiling herself with the swathes of clouds that floated under her. And when he dreamt the action unfolded in her suave light. The moon began to spell security and freedom for him. Through his dreamy states, the moon exercised a subtle power before which even time and space melted away in homage. They presented their faces in discontinuous forms and sounds linked to form a logic of their own, as if to temper their force in respect for her feminine nature.

Chapter 22

An Experience of Death

His dream world did not appear to him as a different plane in total separation from the awakened state. He was indeed the same person in both states. He never experienced the slightest difference between his dream personality and that of his awakened state. Yet the time-space frameworks were never constant either as regards the image and sound entities they engendered or as regards the sequence of events. In his dream world he lived in a completely different universe. The one thing that both had in common was that for the duration of each experience, both he and his world, whatever it was, were experienced as real. In his dream world, the same as in his awakened state, he cried, he laughed, and he felt joy and pain. Depending on the intensity of what he experienced, his dream states endured deep into his awakened life. Often he found himself living with an awakened state body and a dream state mind. That mind too was rooted in the same body. Yet he had a troubling thought about dreams.

Dreams made him understand that his renunciation was not complete. He had even consulted a sage and sought his advice. It was suggested that he undertake some penitentiary practices. He was advised to re-enact his death to this world using other means. One was the undertaking of yatra or pilgrimages. So he decided to go by bus to Devprayag and then on foot to Gangotri.

That night he lay awake on the last step of a ghat staring at the Ganga. When sleep finally came he felt restless especially as he had to get up very early and trudge to the bus stand to take the bus for Devprayag. That night he dreamt again of Maya. She told him she was aware of his plan to proceed to Gangotri and then to

Gaumukh, after which he would proceed to Badrinath. He had remained silent neither confirming nor denying. Maya had gone on speaking but sudden wakefulness had interrupted her discourse. And when renewed sleep overcame his wakeful resistance the dream had disappeared. In the background his friend's voice intoned what had since become the leitmotif of the story of his life: *draw your inspiration from the fire of the pyre.*

****

As the words faded away into the distance he was literally watching his dead body being transferred on a wooden palanquin to the cremation ghat of a place that eluded his mind. His own funeral procession was one among many wending its way through narrow winding lanes while people squeezed themselves on both sides and watched reverently. He heard his bearer incessantly chant: *Rama nama satya hai* – only God is Truth. It brought to his mind the full significance of his life. It had been an illusion all along. It had been a dream. All that mattered was the search of the Eternal and Immortal. The rest was like chaff in the wind, just aimless and incessant drifting from nowhere to nowhere.

The ritual of which he was the object brought to bear on his mind his relationship with the elements. First came the water. His body was submerged in the Ganga. The element of water had played the vital role in his birth being his emergence from the water bag within his mother's womb. Now it was as if he was being confided to the embrace of his mother for the last time in his complete human form. The pyre was now erected and his body placed on it. Then came the turn of fire. The sacred fire was first carried around his pyre three times before it was set alight. He saw the assistants stoking the nascent tongues of fire and maintaining the flames at the greatest possible intensity until his body was reduced to ashes which was the earth element. He felt his flesh crackle and wrinkle like paper as the fire seeped into it and burst out of his mouth, being the final sound he was emitting.

The process went on and on. The assistants were now breaking his bones to make them more easily consumable by the fire. Then finally they cracked open his skull to release his spirit into the great void. He has lost track of time. After what seemed an eternity he felt the fire simmer and subside. He saw his ashes and the left overs of his bones being collected and deposited in the bosom of mother Ganga.

****

The night was very advanced and the darkness was pitch black. The atmosphere was eerie illuminated only by the blazing pyres of varying intensity of light. The air around them had become white with the smoke. The Ganga had itself been rendered invisible behind the smoke screen as if the elements of fire and air had connived to hide the burning bodies from the gaze of the weeping mother. Its course now appeared as tears flowing from sorrowing eyes. The sky was covered by this dense curtain of smoke. All appeared to suggest that nature was sorrowing and weeping while watching the scene. One also saw dogs wandering around the cremation site their noses turned upwards trying to capture each wisp of air bearing the odours that emanated from the burning flesh.

He then saw his self and those of others waiting on the banks of the *Vaitarna*, the eternal river, to be taken across to the other side. But he knew that this was not a one way crossing for him. His soul was stamped with the seal '*I am*', a condition replete with desire that demanded his renewed embodiment in another physical body. He was not standing before a judge who was sentencing him to his fate. It was he who had inscribed his own sentence in his body. As long as his soul was identified with the thought '*I am*' he would cross the *Vaitarna* to and fro relentlessly and endlessly to loan one body after another from the earth. He realized that it was only when his mind was purified of that desire of individual existence embodied by the thought '*I am*' that he could return his body to the earth, discarding it definitively in total settlement of the loan. With his total realization as the One Eternal and Immortal Self his mission of earth would have definitively drawn to and end. But that end was not yet in sight, far from it.

****

There were some matters pertaining to this dream that demanded an explanation. He was dead, cremated and his ashes strewn in the Ganga. He had witnessed everything, yet he was fully conscious. He realized that death had not snuffed out his individual consciousness. He realized that his individual mind was his individual self. He realized that his individual mind and the thought '*I am*' were co-existing features. He realized that death put an end only to his individual physical existence, not to his identity. Yet his identity which had been carried over could not carry on being without the support of a physical body. It had to reemerge anew from within a physical body, growing in unison with it and in dependence on it.

He felt he should probe the matter further and ask himself questions: Awake I have a body and *I am*. Asleep in the dream state I have another body, or no body and *I am*. In deep, dreamless sleep there is no body of which I am conscious of and still *I am*. All these questions and answers led to the irreversible truth, that he was not his body. Such an individual physical existence which he was not had to be an illusion. But so had to be the feeling 'I am' because it existed only in dependence on that particular body and arose out of it. Understanding dawned that a feeling which needed an illusory entity as an integral part of itself for its revival and continuance could itself be nothing else but an illusion. If so his continued existence as an individual was devoid of purpose and finality for what finality could an illusion have? As long as the feeling 'I am' endured his mind would ineluctably and irremediably be linked to a body which was the measure of that feeling.

He realized that he was in the vicious cycle of birth and death, that his mind constituted the hub and the spokes of his wheel of life. He realized that the purpose of life was to shed his illusionary existence. The purpose of life was to escape the claws of this endless cycle of birth and death by realizing his true nature which was within him, which was Eternal and Immortal. That was endless life total, complete and all encompassing, not lived as an illusory one among many, but as the Real One who was the Soul and the Real Identity of the many.

****

At the zenith of this awareness he woke up. He remained affixed to the ground on which he lay, not moving a muscle. He felt himself in the throes of a fear of finding himself in the place, circumstances and surroundings he had experienced during a seemingly incalculable period of time. Then slowly awareness dawned on him that it had all been a dream. How could it be, he spontaneously asked himself, it was so real, so real to feel real. If that was a dream then what is reality? his self questioning continued. That question would linger and demand a solution. But one thing was certain, that death was an illusion.

Indeed how can an illusory entity really die? For all purposes he had experienced death as a reality while his consciousness had remained untouched. It was as if he had come back to his body from a far away realm. He could no more believe his body which was now saying to him that this, his awakened state, was the reality. If that was what his body wanted him to believe then his body was wrong because he knew through experience that his body was not him. If his mind could not exist apart from this illusory body which was not him, then how could such a mind be him? It could not be, indeed it was not. Then who was he?

To find that out he would now have to live in such a way detaching himself both from his body and his mind. He would have to live in the same manner in which a mirror distanced itself from the images it reflected. He realized that thought and emotion personified in the feeling '*I am*' held the key to the problem. He felt his existence as a tug o war between two poles of gravity, the one the Infinite, Eternal and Immortal Divine Awareness and the other the cycle of birth, death and rebirth.

As long as his consciousness was imbued with the 'I am' feeling it would gravitate towards the latter alternative being the cycle of birth and death. Freed from it his consciousness would merge with Divine Awareness. He would have to distance himself from that feeling which was the source of the entire illusion. It arose from his body and stamped itself on his mind. He would now have to escape from its clutches. That was the path to liberation from the endless, purposeless and painful cycle of birth and death.

He had a choice. What was it he wanted: a painful deathlessness of illusory existences, or a blissful end to that illusion by abiding in the Real? Did he want to exist as a temporal, insignificant, senseless, illusory one among many, or did he want to be what he really was, the Eternal, and Immortal of which the one and the many were only illusory manifestations? That was it. He had understood everything. That would henceforward be his only endeavour, his sole and unique purpose in life, to merge with and abide in the Real which was his true nature.

Chapter 23

Phantoms of Memory

While this drama was being staged within him the day had advanced. Passers by threw curious glances at the still figure of the old *sadhu* lying prone on the last step of the *ghat*. Could he be dead? some wondered as they continued on their way. Finally he felt himself being gently shaken by his shoulder. Only then did he open his eyes. '*This is the tenth time I am shaking you*' a gentle voice said. '*I am happy I finally woke you up. We were thinking of carrying you to the pyre! the voice was saying. It is almost nightfall and you can go to sleep again*'. Then he heard a spontaneous sound of laughter accompanying that final phrase. His eyes were wide open now and looking at the sky. Indeed the sky was dark. Was it late evening or early morning he wondered.

His silent question had apparently been carried to the other mind, because he heard the answer. It was as if he was seated at the feet of a guru listening to him discourse. The voice was saying: *what does it matter, morning or night, are they not both the same, just thoughts, just illusions? You were sleeping all this time, did you ever raise the question about day or night? All that happened was that you watched the images and sounds your mind presented before you and to you. Now the stage effects have changed but the mind game will continue. In the world of appearances it is not whether things happen within you or outside of you that is important. It is what the mind presents to you that is important; whether as true or false. Light and darkness are just another set of opposites that change the stage settings. The stage remains the same, the very same. It is like the desert and its mirages. The mirages change, but the desert stays the same. From its fruits you know the nature of the tree. From the nature of the stage effects you know the nature of the stage. Mirages only occur in deserts. Even a desert dreams, and dreams of beautiful gardens, rivers flowing, brooks and waterfalls. Even a desert dreams, and so is the dream of the mind. Distancing oneself from mirages leads to distancing oneself from its source, the mind. Once that awareness dawns the mind will drop. And when the mind drop, all worlds disappear and with them all their frontiers. With no beginning and no end, with no objects, with no frontiers to measure distances and durations will time and space disappear. Only then will your Awareness be Infinite, Immortal and Eternal.*

****

He had remained enthralled and he wanted the voice to continue. Night and day had lost its significance; he just wanted that experience to repeat itself, not once not twice but over and over again. All he wanted now was to die and be reborn during all the eons it could take for him to realize his true Self. He was so possessed of his experience that he did not want to face the world that he would now have to confront with open eyes. He preferred the world he had witnessed behind closed eyes. It had taught him more than the other world had ever done.

He still lingered for a moment in a supine state and finally raised himself up unsure as yet whether he was asleep or awake. As he looked up towards the road, his eye fell on a seated form, a veiled form. It was no doubt a woman. She was holding a baby against her body. She appeared to be looking at him. He slowly walked towards her. As he was about to go past her seized by a sudden desire, he looked into her eyes and immediately recognized her. She was the womanly form of his dreams. She too looked at him with demur eyes and said: *My Baba you were in Samadhi all this while. I saw you, realized it and waited. It was a prolonged dharshan for me. I felt the presence of the divine. It was a blessing for me and our son.*

He stood still for a moment trying to grasp the impact of her words. What did she mean by 'our son'? 'Our son, our son', his mind muttered over and over again without understanding its significance. He looked at them again, the woman and the boy she was carrying. His look was neither one of affirmation nor of denial. He just wanted to tell her to keep silent about him, and she appeared to understand because he saw her looking up at him scrutinizingly before replying: *I promise you Baba, this is our matter and of no one else.* He then stretched out his hand and touched the head of her little son and for once his tongue loosened. *What is his name?* he asked. She looked non-plussed even a little bemused. He saw it in her countenance but did not understand why. *You look surprised at my question* he said. *Why? Baba, my Baba, can you not remember?* she began. Momentarily he held up his hand. It was now his turn to feel perplexed. He had heard himself been addressed with those very words on earlier occasions. The words she had used were stirring his memory, the memory of a dream. His gaze now extended towards the horizon. She thought he was seeing a vision.

****

He felt dizzy and sat on the steps of the *ghat* for a moment of calm. Then his past invaded his mind. He felt wrapped in the folds of the *Badrinath* mountains. He recalled his pilgrimage to that holy city. He had got into a bus at *Rishikesh* heading for *Badrinath.* He ticket collector did not ask him for his ticket money and gave him no ticket either. He had sat next to another *sadhu* also journeying to the same destination. He had journeyed the whole day. They reached the little town well after sun-set. His companion had told him that they could spend their night in an ashram over there. They would go there together. On reaching *Badrinath* they had gone to the temple and after worshipping in the shrine room had taken a bath at the sacred hot water springs. Then they had followed a path at a some what higher level leading into the hills. After a walk of about half an hour they had reached the ashram. The place was full of *sadhus.* Yet they could find enough space to sleep there, the caretaker told them. The alms center attached to the ashram would provide them with food, they were also told.

The next morning he had trudged along the folds of the Himalayas reaching the tapovanam late that evening. He had found shelter under a rocky ledge where he had settled for the night. The space around him was overwhelming. He felt lost in the immensity like a pebble in the bottomless precipices of the Himalayas. Then day broke and the scene imperceptibly changed. He saw himself meditating on the *tapovanam* on the foothills of the *Neelkanth.* How long he had spent up there he could no longer remember. Time had lost every trace of meaning to him. He only saw himself engulfed in an immense void where everything seemed to emerge, change form and disappear into emptiness ablaze with the light of Consciousness. He could not even remember coming down from the mountain. He only recalled what he knew since his childhood about the mountain that it *turned blue at certain times.*

His mind turned narrator continued further. *One must be fortunate to experience that view. It is a dharshan that the Lord gives those who find his favour.* That favour had not come his way, and now it was his last night in the sacred city. *How can I leave without seeing the real colour of the Neelkanth? How can I leave without that dharshan of my Lord?* was the only question that occupied his mind. *Lord*, he said, *I know that I am not worthy. But I will come again. Maybe then you will deign to reveal yourself to your servant.* With that question in mind he had fallen asleep in the open verandah of a shop overlooking the *Neelkanth* .

****

That night his mind was illuminated by a dream. The darkness around him was filled with light and in its midst stood the Lord. He was clothed in the white of the divine glacier and looking benignly down at him. The Lord was saying, *before you go you will have the dharshan you seek. Then you will know that you have found my favour.* Even in his dream he realized that it was his desire that had taken form in his mind. The words of the Lord lingered in him throughout the rest of the night. He woke up early the next morning to catch the bus to *Kashi*. He collected his cloth bag with its weather beaten clothes and stepped out of the shop. He was still in a trance enraptured by the voice his mind had generated in his dream and so did not notice the change in hue in the diluted ambient light.

Then all of a sudden realization came that he was facing the *Neelkanth* and spontaneously he looked up at the peak. To his wonderment and consternation he saw that the peak had turned blue. He felt his knees buckle under him as he fell to the ground and prostrated himself before the heavenly apparition crying out: *Om Namah Shivaya*. He felt himself in the throes of a great emotion and tears of joy were streaming down his cheek. Then as his intense emotion subsided he rose up gazing lovingly at the peak. *Lord* he had muttered, *I have seen your glory: I have seen your glory my Lord, now I can die in peace.*

Hardly had he uttered those words, he saw the mountain metamorphose holding him spell bound. Gently and surely the *Neelkanth* was changing form. Transfixed he was a spectator of a scintillating magical display. The nascent figure that finally burst into view caught him totally by surprise and left him visibly shaken. In the throes of a great emotion he screamed at the sky: *Maya, my never ending dream? Will your memory haunt me till I die?* Her answer filtered through the dense night air: *I am a dream you cannot shake away my baba. But the time of the pursuit is over. This dream is about to become flesh.* He stood watching with glazed eyes hypnotized by what he had seen and heard. When he returned to his senses the mountain had turned marble white as before while what ensued was a disconcerting silence.

****

He was now recalling his journey back from *Badrinath*. Completely engrossed as he was in the divine apparitions and their aftermath, the bus had eluded him that morning. He was advised to proceed on his way with the assurance that some vehicle plying that road would pick him up and take him along. Now he had only the moonlight to contend with. Not being used to the terrain he could not distinguish the main path from the others. After a while he realized that he had gone astray. Fatigue was invading his body especially his legs which were becoming hard like stone. His purpose now was to locate any habitation, any dwelling and the quicker the better it was.

His advance was now becoming laborious. In addition the cough he had developed while on the tapovanam perched midway on his ascent to the *Neelkanth* had aggravated. His cough became louder and appeared to be raking the depths of his lungs. Then once again the thought of death possessed his mind. Unable to proceed he lay on the ground by what appeared to him now to be a vegetable plot. *I am dying but I have seen the dharshan of my Lord*, he heard himself say. *And what about me*? The voice of *Maya* emerged from within him. The *dharshan* of the Lord was for your mind, but I am a dream that can put on flesh. From there on his consciousness vacillated like the flickering light of a candle.

Chapter 24

Recalled to Life

As he dropped down, he felt himself body less on the banks of the river *Vaitarna* looking out for a boat with a ferryman to take him across to the smoke filled ethereal shores of *Vaikuntha*. Then he saw the dark shadow of an old wooden ferryboat looming on the edge of the bank without any boatman in sight. Emaciated as he was he doubted his ability to ferry his boat to the other shore. But something puzzled him. How did he get to the banks of the *Vaitarna* without passing over the pyre? He strained his mind trying to remember and then the semblance of a recollection returned to him.

He saw his funeral pyre blazing against the dark mist covered sky. *Who is doing all this* he had asked himself because he saw his pyre unattended. *Who lit it*, he asked? Then he recalled a faint voice, that of a woman answer. He strained his ears and barely captured the words she uttered but he heard her say: *I*. He had fixed his eyes in the direction from which the voice emanated. As he got used to the eery darkness he had seen a womanly silhouette covered in white that barely distinguished her from the smoke filled surrounding. He saw her seated besides the pyre quietly stirring it and watching it being reduced to ashes. He watched the swirling grey ash flakes disperse until nothing remained. Deep stillness suffused his being as was invaded by the thought that all his connections, yearnings, joys and heartaches had vanished into nothingness. '*This was all there was to it*' he had murmured to himself.

The stillness had expanded and seemed to hold eternity in its embrace. Suddenly he had heard the rustling of a woman's dress near to him. As he got used to the eery darkness he saw a womanly silhouette covered in white that barely distinguished her from the smoke filled surroundings. Slowly the figure had removed the veil from her face and in one instant recognition had dawned: *Maya*, he shouted, *Maya, it is you. Yes me* replied the figure of the woman. *I followed you my Baba. I never left your side. I followed you over the years, and everywhere you went. I saw your body on the banks of mother Ganga with no one to attend to you. It was I who made the pyre and placed you on it. I lit the pyre and am watching as the flames rise towards the sky taking you along with them. Baba, my Baba. I cried the day you left me, I cried as I followed you over the sacred plains and hills during your wanderings. I cried when I saw you seated alone on the banks of the sacred river, alone, yes alone. And now I cry as I see you trying to ferry yourself across the Vaitarna. I will not let you go alone my Baba. I would gladly follow you to where you go, but my time has not yet come. Come back my Baba, come back, to me.* She held out her hand towards him. Maya he cried. *I am coming back to you my love, I am coming back.* As he spoke he saw the whitish lumpings of ash strewn on the site of his pyre levitating in a terrifying whirl and re-assuming his physical form.

****

You are going no where, you are staying where you are. He heard the same womanly voice say authoritatively. *How did you know my name* she was asking him? *You said Maya several times. That is me. I am Maya. Maya means illusion. Tonight there is the moon, the full moon. Do you remember what I told you in that train, the day you left your home? One day by the light of the moon we will unite and I will never leave you again my baba. Tonight the moon is all aglow. You are going to get well my Baba. I am going to nurse you back to good health. No you are not going anywhere anymore. You are staying with me.* Where am I, he finally asked? I remember descending the Neelkanth mountain and making my way out of the town. It was dark and I could not see. I remember descending a long path that appeared to be leading nowhere. That is all I remember. She replied: *I saw you approach and I watched you from within my hut. Then I saw you collapse coughing violently all the time. That was a long time ago. I have been nursing you since then. Today you are having high fever and fell into a state of delirium. It is then that I heard you talk, calling to me...yes to me by name, Maya. You said, Maya, I am coming back to you my love, I am coming back. You recognized me. Our story has a very long past.*

He looked at her noticing the bulge of her stomach indicating that she was with child. For the first time since he assumed the life of a wanderer he felt a surge of love for her, for this apparition that had long been haunting his dreams. He took her hand in his, the hand of the woman who had nursed him back to life. *I do not remember when, where and how. But this I know, I have been away from you for a very long time and now I have come back to you.* She shuddered as she felt a shock wave going through her spine. She closed her eyes enjoying the feeling of his hand in hers. That night and every subsequent night she slept next to him enfolding him in her arms trying to give him the added warmth of her own body. As her stomach pressed against his side he felt movements from within it. It was the child as if reacting to a paternal presence it had not enjoyed before.

Then the voice of long ago emerged as a deep vibration from the depths of his memory and burst into his mind as sound. Do you remember *that night our mutual ecstasy bore fruit my baba? That fruit is leaping for joy sensing your presence. How do you intend calling your child?* he asked. *Our child my baba*, she corrected him without any sentiment of reproach. *I have not given him a name yet, Baba* said the young mother. *What should I call him?* she asked enquiringly. His mind aglow with the *dharshan* of the lord of the mountain he answered: *If a boy, call him Neelkanth, if a girl, call her Anandamayi*, There was a moment's silence.

Then she spoke again. *Neelkanth is the Lord, Anandamayi means joy. What if it is a boy?* She insisted. *Then it will be you, Anandamayi*, he replied softly.

****

It took him a short time to re-find his bearings after the mental turbulence he had undergone, still totally unsure in which state he was. And when the calm descended once again he looked at her and remembered. It was the womanly form that had kept him company since the day he left his home. Indeed his dream had taken flesh as the woman he had noticed following him on the outskirts of the Luxman Jhula bridge, the woman who had given him shelter from the pouring rain. Finally, after a long reflective pause, his pensive face assumed the traits of paternal tenderness. And then he spoke. *This is Neelkanth*, he said touching the head of the little boy. *And I am Maya*, she said softly. No, he answered determinedly, *you were Maya, now you are Anandamayi, you are Joy.* Holding her boy fast to her breast, she knelt before him and touched his feet. He heard her whisper to her son: *did you see him my son? The Baba is your father you are Neelkanth. That is your name my baby, the name he gave you. You are Neelkanth his son, the son of the Enlightened one. He left us a long time ago my baby but for a just cause. He left us to find deliverance. He has found it. Now he has come back to us.*

As he left the scene he thoughts lingered over a sage of a very long time ago who had left his young wife and newborn babe to find deliverance. And then he came back to see them. *How would that meeting have been?* he wondered. *That mother's name too was Maya, and her little boy would have been of the same age as Neelkanth.*

Chapter 25

A Joyful Reunion

He felt his strength failing him. He was now eighty-five which meant that seventeen years had elapsed since he made his great renunciation. He had now reached a stage in his life when dream state and awakened state constantly merged transforming his life into one uninterrupted, endless vision. Whatever he did that was of an exceptional nature, he recalled to mind at will and relived it incessantly. One such was his voyage to *Gangotri* and from there to the *Gaumukh* and to the *Tapovanam* lying several kilometers above it. He had undergone experiences of this nature on several occasions and his yearning to be there again grew with every passing day.

And so he left his seat on the *ghat* and made his way along well known roads and paths. He had the distinct impression that this was a journey dictated by the unseen force of destiny, and that destiny had something unexpected in store for him. The journey took much longer than on previous occasions. He felt his body straining to the utmost under the weight of age. On this occasion, more than ever, he felt the reverence and affection of which he was the object on the part of all: it was as if all wished to participate in his journey by contributing in some way to its success. Everyone seemed to instinctively know where the old *sadhu* was heading for. Everyone seemed to sense that this was the journey of his life. Everyone seemed to want to die and be reborn through him. Everyone was considering him as the gateway to another life, to a better one.

****

Then one day on a very cold morning, he found himself standing in front of the rocky outcrop, the *gaumukh*, serving as outlet for the waters of the *Baghirathi*. Standing in the basin like contour of the site and seeing the Holy Ganges trickle out as water that had sprung out of its source the melting glacier, he sensed his body liquefy and being carried away by the streamlet. He had felt the water ablaze with light, its shimmering glittering surface expanding and flowing over the four horizons. His experience was of oneness with the water, one with its sanctity. He did not realize where he was or that time was passing. He was experiencing the immensity within himself, an immensity that had stretched the contours of his physical self to the utmost limits of the horizon and beyond, into the unperceivable, incomprehensible, and unfathomable. He had become THAT, the ineffable mystery of limitless enlightened awareness.

When he came back to himself, he sensed that he was not alone. There was a group around him. They were staring at him while maintaining a healthy distance from him. Some were in the act of worshiping him. Others were intoning the mantra: *Nama Shivaya*. Yet he did not feel being an object of contemplation by 'others' and venerated by them. What he perceived was forms, movements and sound with which he shared all in the joy of being one, He smiled and they smiled back. Once the moment of amazement was over, they asked him, where he was heading for. He replied, the *Tapovanam. We are going there* they said. They were almost entreating him to come along. They helped him along the way, pausing with him every time he needed a rest. They had abandoned their usual youthful banter as if awe struck by his presence and not willing to profanate it with worldly sounds. And then with a final tug they heaved him over and on to the *Tapovanam*. There they worshipped him and left him to his own.

****

Flowing through the *Tapovanam* meadow in small outflows was the *Aakash Ganga* the waters of which formed small pools in some areas of the plateau aided by the appropriate rock formations. If there was a place which filled the mind with a sense of the eternal, it was this. Strewn over this extensive Himalayan mountain shelf were rudimentary huts built on prop up supports which sheltered ascetics in search of the eternal and the undying. Some of these shelters seemed embedded in rocky outcrops which ensured more stability.

The living area of these ascetics, called *kuttis* were small and surrounded with thick material to ensure some semblance of warmth for their occupants. There were also the low flat tents of tourists who had undertaken the arduous ascent from the *Gaumukh* rock. Some wanted to bathe in the breath taking mountain landscape. Others were intent on obtaining a spiritual life transforming experience enabling them to see life for what it was, a transient speck of the infinite. He recalled what he had heard during his ascent from *Gangotri* to *Gaumukh*. Someone had described the human person as a pebble lost in the bottomless depths of the Himalayan precipices, as one indistinguishable from the rest, as one who could be any other and every other. That was indeed why he was born, to lose himself in the bottomless depths of Infinite Awareness.

****

As night approached he was seeking out a place of rest. So worn out he had no strength to construct a rudimentary enclosure for himself as protection against the powerful winds and the biting cold. He just lay on his back on the bare ground and wrapped himself as well as he could. The excessive cold and the powerful winds kept him awake for some time. Then his body overcome by fatigue resorted to a ploy to induce sleep. He began to feel that he was in a train. The winds striking against the mountain slopes now seemed to him like the rattling of the train as it heaved from side to side weaving its way across the plains. Then the sounds were transformed into voices, and the voices put on a form. It was the form of his friend. He was now seated beside him in the train speaking of the goals he should strive to attain as a sannyasi. *Go to the sources of the waters. They are all in the hills. The source of water is in the hills. When you reach its source stillness prevails. Seek the company of those who live in stillness and silence. They are like the mountain sources of the waters where the water is pure and not contaminated by the impurities it accumulates on the way...and maybe one night on awakening you might find me.*

He appeared to be dozing when he heard a voice that seemed to emerge from his far away dreams. That voice was repeating the very same phrase. The timber and quality of the voice was different and shook him awake. What he was seeing was a *sadhu* bending over him and inviting him to his *kutti*. *You will not survive this frosty wind and biting cold*, he was saying, *come inside my tent*. He felt frozen but not for the cold. His entire body strained to identify that voice. And then like a thunder clap the words struck him: *Pahar Ganj*, That was where he had heard it for the last time. *What I hear is the voice of a god*, he uttered overcoming his incredulity. There was a moment's silence as the other tried to find his bearings, and then the words gushed joyous, almost ecstatic. *Now I can die in peace, I have seen your face again*, he said. It was only then that the other spoke. *I came here longing for your dharshan. This moment my desire has been realized. Did I not tell you when we last met that*: *maybe one night on awakening you might find me*?

It was with great love that the two friends embraced, just as they did for what was deemed to be the last time at the *Pahar Ganj* station. *You look so pulled down and tired*, his friend said. *I will look after you*. That night after partaking of a meal of lentils and chapati with the hot steaming tea that followed all prepared by his friend on make shift material, he slept a dreamless sleep. He spent the next few days in deep communion with his friend. They talked over many things, especially their experiences of the ascetic life. Then the conversation veered to the life of the *rishis* of the *Tapovanam*.

Chapter 26

Unanswered Question

In the tapovan no one knows what is passing through the minds of the meditating *Rishis*. Yet people venerated them. They did so with their own preconceived ideas. Everyone attributed to the *rishis* their own spiritual goals and thought they were been accomplished by the rishis on their behalf, his friend said. However, he added, what one experiences in the high sphere of detachment and renunciation is anyone's guess.

On hearing this, he asked: *how could the mind comprehend such an experience, leave alone translating it into words?* That is not possible was the reply. To support his contention his friend was reciting the words of the Upanishads: *There the eye goes not, Speech goes not, nor the mind. We know not, we understand not, how would one teach it?*

The merging with Divine Awareness surpassed the capacities of the mind to comprehend and to elucidate. It was simply ineffable and that being the case, people surrounding holy men begin attributing to them their own ideologies and religiosity. As for the holy men themselves, they are uneasy with words. They consider words as traps. They have their conventional content which is totally insufficient to express strictly personal spiritual experiences. The innermost state of being they experience they cannot convey. Both fell silent for a moment. Finally he broke the silence with the observation: *the only refuge for a holy man is silence.*

Yet some did speak and when they did they often expressed themselves differently. They claimed to have been in total possession of All, yet expressed themselves and lived each his own way. Some were even respectfully critical of one another. There was no inalienable togetherness of all, in all, and with all. The surpassing of the frontiers of the senses and of the mind did not manifest itself through them through the same universality of expression and of living. Each retained his individuality and is otherness.

He could only conclude that not only could an individual person not express the totality of his God experience, but that such an experience while retaining even some semblance of relationship to the physical body and mind could not be total, but adapted to the condition of the body and its mind. A human body was absolutely unique in the entire history of space and time. It was absolutely individual and personal, non imitable and non transferable. This uniqueness was evident in the ways the body acted and reacted in relation to the impulses of the mind. That would also necessarily be the case with regard to experience and expression of such experience of Divine awareness by the enlightened mind. He even wondered whether such an experience could ever be total during an individual's lifetime. Such was the greatness and glory of God in comparison with an entity that had traversed his allotted temporal-spatial distance with all the limitations of his temporal-spatial nature. This doubt even found expression in the holy Vedic texts:

Who truly knows, who can honestly say where this universe came from and where it will vanish to at the End? Those godlike wise men who claim they know were born long after the birth of Creation. Who then could know where our universe really came from? And whoever knows or does not know where Creation came from, only one gazing at its vastness from the very roof of the final Heaven "Only such a one could possibly know, but does even He know?"

Apart from faultless lives and dedication to humanity, there could be no other proof of their claim of experiencing oneness with the Divine nature, of realization of the same divine Self. Each of them would have a devoted following of disciples, close and distant. They would also have contestants of their claims. Some were destined to be worshipped as the manifestations or revelations of the Living God. *Samadhis* would come up over their tombs and temples would be erected in their honour. Eventually priests would appear on the scene and perform rituals and rites of purification, of cleansing and healing, in their name. Others would follow the paths of lesser mortals.

****

Our life as renouncers has only one goal, the achievement of *Samadhi* and continuance in that state. We have strained every nerve and sinew to that end, he said. His friend's reply opened his eyes to other perspectives of that search. The experience of Samadhi, as you surely know, is not necessarily the culmination of a life time of sustained effort at its realization. It could happen to anyone, anywhere and for a multitude of reasons. It had happened to one great bhagavan when he was only sixteen years old and as a result of his simulating death with intent to get rid of the fear of it. Others have had the *samadhi* experience both in India and abroad in circumstances that do no necessarily indicate a life style of self negation and sacrifice. *What is the basic explanation for these differences*? he enquired.

A particular circumstance called upon to explain such situations is the law of *karma*. We are, says this law, the most recent link in a long chain of rebirths. We are, it is said, creatures of our thoughts and actions. Our good *karma* finds recompense in this life while the bad have to be atoned in various ways. For instance the untimely death of a virtuous person is ascribed to bad karma of the past. So too whatever be the age or condition of life of an individual, he could experience the blissful state of *samadhi* through energies arising from good *karma* of the past.

The past, the past, he said, *everything about it is so unclear, just the unending whirl of matter leaving our imagination to give it the form it deems fit. Indeed imagination was the pillar of support of faith and belief*. Normal life for the ordinary human person as conceived within his belief structure, is full of inputs from previous births of which the person is unaware of and unconscious. This also means that his present existence is formed from thoughts and deeds of other times and other spaces. As said in the sacred writings of one religion: "*We are what we think, having become what we thought*."

Thought then is the creator of the scenario in which we live, not only the thoughts of this existence but all thoughts of our entire chain of existences. We are either floating or floundering on an ocean of our own thoughts. In other words our actual life is but a wave on an ocean of ever dominant and self producing thoughts. *But what is our actual life*, he asked. Every life we live we experience as such, as an actual life, as the one and only one. We have never known any other. No, we have never known any other and our closest approximation of knowing any others is our dreams.

He even wondered, considering that every life lived was unique and irretrievable, whether the self would ever know of its absorption into Eternal, Immortal and Infinite Awareness. He even dared to question whether such a consciousness too was only a dream and a myth. He knew he would have to face the event of his death. But how would he know he had died? He had seen others die, and knew how their bodies were disposed, but he would never know such circumstances in his own regard. He only knew his awakened state and his dream state with fluctuations in between. In his awakened state he made use of a body, but so did he also in his dream state. The body served the purposes of each state though it was not the same body.

The body of his dream state served all the purposes of the dream. Now what if death was a deep sleep and a long dream? Would he feel the lack of the body he used in his awakened state? Or would the disappearance of the body of his wakened state also put an end to the body of his dream state? He did not know. He just knew he would never know that he was dead. That was what others would know of him but not he. And then the other question rose. And what they would know, could it also be their dream? their myth? Suddenly another thought struck him: when death did come, how would he know that he was no more? How would others know because if he was no more the others too would cease to be. It all seemed so funny that he burst out laughing. He laughed and laughed until tears streamed down his cheeks. When calm descended he said: *if not for dreams, life would be a joke*!

The endeavour of all our lives then is to see. Finally it is that we see that matters and not how we see. He recalled the question of a prophet to a blind man. *What do you wish that I do to you? Lord that I may see*, the man had replied. The reality of vision overshadows every other as shown by that once blind man's words to those who assailed him with questions. *Only this I know, that whereas I was blind, now I see.* Yes, and what more joy, bliss and ecstasy than to behold the giver of sight?

****

He had decided to leave the next morning. He had spent his day meditatively walking on the high plateau. His entire life had filtered through his mind in a final review. He had looked up now and then and seen and sensed the majestic mountains that stretched skywards all around him like silent sentinels, witnesses to that all powerful and all encompassing Divine Awareness. That night he laid his shaggy rug outside his cave and sat cross legged on it. Then overcome by an insurmountable feeling of awe at the grandiose landscape that surrounded him he broke into prayer with the words:

O Lord, my God, when I in awesome wonder, Consider all the works Thy hand hath made, I see the stars, I hear the mighty thunder, Thy power throughout the universe displayed;

When through the woods and forest glades I wander, And hear the birds sing sweetly in the trees; When I look down from lofty mountain grandeur, And hear the brook, and feel the gentle breeze; Then sings my soul, my Lord, my God, to Thee, How great Thou Art! How great Thou Art!

****

That whole night he seemed to hear a voice surging from within him with the same question: what do you wish, to be One with me, or to see me...what do you want, to be One with Me or to see Me? Feeling compelled to give an answer to that question that kept repeating itself inexorably, he said: *Lord, give me time, I pray Thee give me time.* He heard the voice reply: that time is limited, your days are numbered. Your time of choice is now, after that it will be as it is.

Then the time came for him to go. This final separation was a moment of anguish which he strove valiantly to overcome. *On both occasions it is I who leave you*, he told his friend as they embraced for the last time. His friend kept watching him descend as long as he was within his field of vision. He left the tapovanam in a completely different frame of mind as from the last occasion. On the previous occasion he was One with the Eternal and Immortal. But now he felt his mind tossed on waves of uncertainty. What did he want, to see God in an unending dharshan or to be One with God by merging in Divine Awareness? He could not answer. His entire education, his upbringing and spiritual training and striving made him tend towards the latter. Yet that striving was questioned by an innate yearning of his heart, to see the One he had tried to unite with in a life long endeavour. The answer given by the blind man to the prophet rang in his mind: *Lord that I may see.*

Chapter 27

A Review of Life

He felt the end was approaching and with it the urge to review his life. He tried to trace it back as far as it went. The returns were nevertheless so meager, just a handful of images on one scale of his balance of life as against his eighty five years on the other. His entire life had been miniaturized into a handful of flash cards. He also recalled it being said of dying persons that their entire life flashed across the scene of their consciousness. He tried to rationalize that saying: what could that be, an entire life time flashing before the dying person's mind? What else he said, but a drowning man grasping at his personal identity as the last straw that life could offer him. And what a straw at that, a scene as one on a digital flash card, a mere nothingness, an illusion a non-reality, a dream.

He remembered a paragraph written in his personal diary of long ago. *This morning I awoke to the sound of birdsong and it sounded exactly the same as the birdsong that I would hear outside my window as a child. And in that moment, time dissolved. I realized that nothing had changed — nothing. The singer appeared the same, the song as well and also the listener. Where were the several decades of distance that separated the two in time and space? The sameness of the forms and the sounds had obliterated both in the twinkling of an eyelid. He realized that it was the mind the magician.* It was the mind that caused the distances, and it was the mind that effaced them. The more he advanced in age the more times and places presented themselves as broken bits and pieces like in the hands of a juggler. Consciousness was now acting as a juggler throwing them up for his viewing and reviewing in an unassorted and in a disconnected, haphazard, chaotic and topsy turvy manner. His world had suddenly become the stuff that dreams are made of.

Then he heard the voice of the waters. He was as usual seated on the last step of the ghat when that voice pierced through the turmoil in his mind. *Put your hand in me*, the voice was saying. He obeyed as instructed, *What do you feel*, the voice of the river asked him. I feel your flow, he answered. *Now withdraw your hand* was the next command. He did so, and heard the implacable voice ask: *Do you feel my flow now?* No, he answered. *You have placed yourself outside the flow of time. Get inside the flow and you will feel the flow, get outside it, and that sensation ceases to be.* Once in the flow one feels the full weight of time in all its ramifications, but once outside it its divisions disappear, as also what once seemed to be its sacrosanct and overpowering content. He recalled the lines uttered by the bard:

"Our revels now are ended. These our actors,
As I foretold you, were all spirits and
Are melted into air, into thin air:
And, like the baseless fabric of this vision,
The cloud-capp'd towers, the gorgeous palaces,
The solemn temples, the great globe itself,
Yea, all which it inherit, shall dissolve
And, like this insubstantial pageant faded,
Leave not a rack behind. We are such stuff
As dreams are made on, and our little life
Is rounded with a sleep."

There was nothing more that life could offer him as reality. It had necessarily to be a dream.

****

That night the Ganges came alive. All whom he had loved and known appeared to him in the flowing waters that assumed their forms. They looked lovingly at him. And when the procession seemed to be over, he heard the sound of the waters: *tonight you will see me again...tonight you will see me again....tonight you will see me again...*the soothing sound of the waters said over and over again, before adding, *then you will decide on the answer to my question*. He decided to sit through the night with all alertness to see the ultimate manifestation of God. Yet without his knowledge he fell into a deep sleep. Even in his sleep his subconscious seemed to be awake, for it repeated over and over again to him: *stay awake, stay awake, He is coming...He is coming, and you will see him as he wishes that you see Him.*

****

Lapsing into a reverie he asked himself: *where have all the years gone? Look at me, my white hair, my white beard, my wrinkled skin, my drawn features!* The answers arose like the ripples of the waters he was looking into. Tell me, those ripples were asking him. How do you count time? *By the seconds, the minutes, the days, the weeks the months, the years, the eons.* Stop stop, the ripples told him laughing merrily. Let us consider the last, the eons. How do you conceive an eon? He was stuck for an answer. I will tell you, a ripple continued: it is at the most a blurred image of your imagination. In how much time would you conceive that image? *In no time* he ventured to reply. Now how would you conceive hundreds of eons, nay thousands of them? Still the silence prevailed. You seem embarrassed to answer, ripple said. Well, its just the same, a blurred image of your imagination conceived in no time. So much time, endless time and conceived in no time! So funny, she said. What followed were ripples of laughter.

Listen well, the ripple told him. When the mind is stretched beyond its measure, time and space are obliterated. Both stand and fall together. Also remember, you can neither go backwards nor forwards even a second in time. If that is your condition in time, so it also is with space. You think your life has taken so much time and covered so much distance. But when you look back you have to say, *it all happened in no time*: indeed in no time and in no space. All that remains is that blurred image, a construct of your imagination. Do not look at yourself from outside of you and be deceived, because time and space is the mirror of illusion. You have aged in the mirror or time and space. Look within you and be aware of the ageless one that you are. Now we must go they said, there is much more to follow. He thought of the words of the English bard who had imbibed his wisdom in India: we seem to turn the wheel on which we turn but still that wheel is forever still.

****

He was now watching the gentle ripples move on after having imparted this sublime teaching. It was then that the sound of the river began to change as it had done once before. The noise of the waters became louder and louder. The phenomenon he had witnessed once before was happening again. The waters whirled and twirled at lightening speed groaning and foaming in a scintillating display that was absolutely fascinating and breathtaking to watch. When the noises and the whirling subsided and came to a stop what emerged was the beauteous figure of the young god of time and of the waters.

Shiva, Shiva he shouted with unbridled enthusiasm and joy. You said you would return and you have come back. You said you would return and you have come back. I have many things to ask you. Lord, I am now a very old man. I have trudged and trekked the mighty landscapes of the Land of the Gods. I have moved over vast expanses mostly on foot. I have covered enormous distances in search of the ONE, the Eternal, the Infinite, the Immortal. The Lord who listened patiently then said: *The self of each and everyone results from the conjuring tricks of the great hypnotizer that is Maya. So are also the exploits of the 'self' you have enumerated: the trudging, the trekking, the moving on and the covering of those mighty and vast expanses. A self abiding in the ONE does not move and inch. He goes nowhere. He is always HERE.*

Those words of the Lord struck a chord in his mind. Those were the very words Bhagavan Ramana Maharshi told an English lady on hearing her say that she had come a long way to see him. He replied: *you have not moved an inch.* The Bhagavan had described life abiding in the SELF or in Divine Consciousness as a 'waking sleep'. Experiencing the utter peace and care-free bliss of formless deep sleep the Divine Consciousness was clearly aware of the power emanating from it resulting in the arising forms. How can a person enjoying such a formless deep sleep move even an inch? How can the awareness of arising forms move him? As in life, so also it was in death. On his death bed, the same Bhagavan told his devotees: *they say I am dying, that I am going away, but where am I to go. I am* HERE. His thoughts dwelt on the ocean depths unfathomable distances below the surface that remained unmoved, immovable, and impenetrable as if in deep formless sleep, while waves arose and fell way above it and in dependence on its sheer power. Overwhelmed by this thought he heard himself murmuring the lines of a prayer: *O strength and Stay upholding all creation Who ever dost Thyself unmoved abide, yet day by day the light in due gradation from hour to hour through all its changes sustain.*

He was now listening to his mind speak and rationalize that spiritual experience. You were a teacher of philosophy and religions. A great Greek philosopher said: no one bathes twice in the same river. A great religious teacher went even farther. He said: the person who gets into the same river twice is not the same person. Everything within us and outside us is in the throes of incessant change. There is no one to go anywhere and there is no where for anyone to go. If everything is in a permanent state of flux, if there is absolutely nothing that is immobile, there is no measure of movement and distance. Movement and distance thus become empty feelings and concepts evanescent in nature.

Everything within and outside each and everyone is subject to inexorable change. Birth, growth, decay and death is the common lot. The only unchangeable, immovable is the Eternal, Immortal and Infinite Self which is ONE in all. The words of the Lord bore deep into his mind. He knew the Self he always sought was always within him. It was not an object to be sought such as the Holy Grail or the Golden Fleece. The paramount goal of his life was to merge his consciousness with the Awareness of the Self that he always had been. But now time was running out.

My strength is failing rapidly and I wish to know what you foresee of my future. *I see you have not understood my words of the last occasion. The past is what counts. The farthermost past is the beginning, so is the utmost end. Everything begins all the time. Do not think in terms of past, present and future, think rather in terms of beginning.* The words of the Lord were profound in their connotation. Lord he asked full of apprehension. Am I going to die? The infectious smile on the face of the Lord continued: *Death comes to those who think they exist. But for those who know that individual existence or life is no more real than a reflection in a mirror, or the mirage that is space-time, there is no death and no dying. In this cycle of infinite life, in this cycle in which what goes around comes around, birth and death are illusions.*

You called yourself an inveterate dreamer and so you have been. You then know that life is a dream, the stuff of myths. You are the story of a dream, the dream of the UNBORN. So how can you die? He listened but was still full of apprehension. Tell me Lord, what is death? *You sleep do you not? Is not an exhausted old man overcome by sleep? Sleep is the land of dreams. Is not dreaming a bewildering experience? So you will sleep, and in your sleep you will continue to dream.* He felt his fears were calmed. Lord I feel strengthened and comforted by your words. Yes I waited for the night to engulf me and so usher me into the world of sleep and dreams. It is through my dreams that I brought out the best in me. My dreams were my psychologists, my doctors, my teachers. My dreams provided me with love and understanding. You tell me that I will sleep and that I will dream. Now I fear nothing.

May I ask you a final question my Lord? The young God was looking at him encouragingly. Lord, will I be reborn? *Oh,* the Lord said, *is it that that worries you now? You think you are old, you are dying...but your mind still has the traits of a child! I think I have told you enough for you to elicit your own answer.* Noting the silence that followed the Lord asked: *Have you forgotten what I told you during our last encounter?* I said: *I came to tell you not to search for time in the present or the future. Time is embodied in the past. Your question suggests you still consider rebirth to be a future state of life. It furthermore contains a latent and implicit preoccupation going to the root of the entire issue. That unnamed but obvious apprehension is induced by fear: the anguish of becoming 'another' and losing the 'self' you are presently conscious of and with which you identify your existence.*

Let me answer these two questions, the overt first question and the latent second. Rebirth is an ongoing process of which you are unwittingly and unknowingly the actor and the sufferer. You are both the container and the content of the simultaneous overlapping ebb and flow of life, of being and becoming at one and the same time. As regards the second issue, your much vaunted 'self' to which you are attached more than to life itself is a myth. What you fear of losing is nothing but a transient evanescent feeling which your mind has converted into a hardened immobile and immovable entity. Still deeper, that agony is all about relinquishing your body the source of all your feelings. Yet none of all these factors is 'you': none of them is yours. Your attitude is much akin to that of a desert laying claim to a mirage or a dreamer laying claim to a dream.

Therefore I am telling you once again that the present is only the continually and interminably unfolding past. Rebirth is nothing other than calling yourself out of that nebulous zone in the depths of the inexhaustible ocean of story onto its glimmering ever unfurling waves that you claim as being the present. Your past is that unidentifiable mask to which you feel irrevocably and irremediably attached while the present is your futile illusory and endless effort to fit and adjust it with a face which you can identify as being yours and call your 'self'. In the final result you are just what your mind says that you are, whatever be the self invented partition of time you project yourself into. Anyway, just close your eyes and you will see for yourself. Just tell me when you have had enough of it, were the last words the Lord said, not without a tinge of mischief.

He did as he was told. For a second everything was still. Then he felt himself as being in the throes of change. His consciousness was being flooded by wave after wave of incessant images. He was continuing to be himself but as another and yet another and yet another. It was as if his form was being drawn on quick sands, incessantly taking shape and incessantly disappearing. In that ocean of change he was clutching on to what appeared to his mind to be two buoys: memory and imagination.

They were presenting to him an ever changing landscape, environment and network of imagery that gave apparent stability and continuity to his form that kept appearing and subsiding on the quick sands of time and space. He was living in his mind. He felt himself being ever the same, but yet he was another and yet another and yet again another. He felt himself personified within a body that was being born, that progressed in age, then decayed and disappeared. He felt himself in a trance while what was happening continued unabated. He felt himself as if balanced on a sea-saw of transitory joys and happiness on the one hand and enduring remorse and regrets, both sources of suffering, on the other.

And so the waves of becoming and coming into being as an ever changing 'other' with that ever enduring feeling of being himself went on and on over what seemed to be the oceans of incalculable time and unending space but which were nothing but an unending here and now. He was as if in a deep sleep, but this dream, this continuous occurrence was not asleep. He was experiencing a 'waking sleep'. How long this went on he did not know.

Mesmerized, hypnotized, transfixed by the seemingly inexorable ongoing process, his mind was enmeshed in the prison of his senses and wallowing in it. Maya and mara were the spokes and the reel that held the wheel of becoming in place. Above the turmoil voices arose trying to make themselves heard, and filtered through his subjugated mind. One voice which evoked a drama he had witnessed in his youth was saying: *You know and do not know, what it is to act or suffer. You know and do not know, that acting is suffering, and suffering action.*

In the drama of his life he was never an indifferent observer. He was either the consenting subject or the patient object of an unfolding action. As long as he rode the wheel of maya that action that enfolded him in either capacity would be seeped in suffering. Yet his consent and patience would serve as buffers against the pain that was his lot. He felt like a boxer in a ring, giving and receiving blows, but relieved by the wet towels of consent and acceptance which his seconds, his senses, were covering him with.

All this while the wheel relentlessly dragged him through its eternal rotations. That wheel of birth, death and rebirth, the stage of the hallucinating dance of maya with its lightning gyrations hid the truth from him. That truth was, that the wheel that appeared to be turning was nevertheless still for forever, that the ocean that moved in waves on the surface buffeted by the winds and currents, nevertheless remained immobile and unmoved in its fathomless ineffable depths. The commotion and pandemonium that reigned within him could not suppress that truth which stood above the din. And so he heard it said: *O strength and Stay upholding all creation Who ever dost Thyself unmoved abide.* Indeed maya had no power except what had been imparted to her by that force of creation which itself abided unmoved.

So the struggle of life and death continued unabated until he heard the Lord's voice. *Break off man, break off man*, the Lord was shouting. *Finish off with it. Do you not see that birth, death and rebirth is an ongoing process even in what you consider to be your unique life time. Do you not realize that it is suffering? that it takes you nowhere?that it is vain? Wake up and abide in your real Self. Stop being another and another like the ever rising waves of the ocean. You are not a wave, you are the ocean of BEING. You are THAT, the Eternal, Infinite, Immortal Divine Consciousness.*

He was now looking into the eyes of the God. They were filled with love. *Lord*, he said, *abide with me*, and his lips moved in prayer, intoning a hymn he had learned in his childhood: *Abide with me; fast falls the eventide; the darkness deepens; Lord, with me abide. When other helpers fail and comforts flee, Help of the helpless, O abide with me. Swift to its close ebbs out life's little day; earth's joys grow dim; its glories pass away; change and decay in all around I see; O thou who changest not, abide with me.*

Then as he watched, the young god leaned out of the waters towards him and took him in his arms in a tender, loving embrace. His parting words were: *fear not: I will be revealing myself to you again tonight, and you will know that you have dreamt the right dreams and your dreams have borne fruit*. He closed his eyes savouring every moment of what was happening to him. Then he heard the droning sound of the waters. When he opened his eyes, he saw the Ganges flowing gently at his side.

Chapter 28

Final Revelation of God

Is not an exhausted old man overcome by sleep? and in your sleep you will continue to dream, he said recapitulating the words of the god. He had felt the embrace of God and heard his consoling words, now all he wanted was to fall asleep in his arms. And with that thought he dozed off. *You have dreamt well, your dreams have borne fruit* were the next words he heard as sleep took over.

How long he slept he did not know. In his dream state his mind was conjuring up a scene from the past. He felt himself lying in a ramshackle shelter in a lofty mountainous region, waiting for dawn to catch the bus that would bring him down to the plains. He felt the time ticking by at an incredibly slow pace and heard himself murmuring: *Creator of the earth and sky, Oh tell my why you made this night go slowly, while here I lie, so sleepless, old and weary*. He then suddenly felt shaken out of his reverie by what he was seeing. Rising steeply in front of him was the Neelkanth glacier the marble like whiteness of which was changing hue and turning blue. The colour change had now reached its climax but the transformation was not over.

What he saw next made him gasp for breath. The mountain was melting making the blue peak shrink beyond recognition and assume diminutive proportions. And now the bulge that remained was shuddering and trembling much like the contractions of a womb at child birth. It seemed to him that the divinity of the mountain was breaking himself free from his confines and struggling to be reborn in an avatar of his choice. What emerged from this hallucinating spectacle was the form and figure of a little boy. He was clad in a little blue short and a blue shirt to match while a blue school bag dangled behind his shoulders. Stunned and shocked as he was his mind was straining to the utmost trying to unravel the mystery unfolding before him.

But all of a sudden he was awakened by noises. He knew that the Lord was coming back to him and his eyes focused on the waters eager to see the form in which God would be revealing himself. What the waters were presenting to his view was the nearby school from where the noises were emanating. The noises were those of children who were leaving its precincts and heading towards their loved ones waiting for them outside. Then he heard a well known voice shouting out to him and saw the little blue clad boy of his dream of a while ago running towards him, his little school bag dangling on his back, his arms stretched in expectation of his embrace. The little voice was shouting: *papaji, papaji, papaji*.

His face beamed with delight and a feeling of love rarely sensed before, invaded his entire being. In the background of his mind the lines of the God were still playing like background music. *You have dreamt well and your dreams have borne fruit*. He saw his little boy and sensed an upsurge of joy which thrilled him. *Neelkanth, Neelkanth* he was shouting back at the rapidly advancing little figure. *Neelkanth my son, Neelkanth my little boy, wait, I am coming, I am coming*. In his sleep and with outstretched arms he took a few laboured halting steps on the sloping *ghat* all ready to take the little figure in his arms in an ardent paternal embrace. Then he heard a splash and shuddered as the cold waters engulfed him, and the night fell.

****

That night *Maya* was troubled in her sleep by a foreboding. Finally dozing off through sheer fatigue she was awakened by a knock on her door. When she opened it she saw Ganga baba standing on the threshold with his meager belongings thrust under his armpit. He said *I came to see you and our son*. Why at the dead of night my Baba she asked surprised. He smiled, stepped in and went to where the boy was sleeping. He knelt down by his side and touched his head in a gesture of protection. Then turning to her he said: *I have seen you both, now I am happy, now I can go*. Go where, go where my baba she cried out: I will follow you to the end of the earth. Wait, she pleaded stretching her hand towards him in a supplicatory gesture with tears welling in her eyes. He looked at her with great tenderness and then made ready to leave. Then she gathered her clothes around her, rose up, and rushed to him, knelt down and placed her head on his feet reminiscent of the gesture of his wife the day he left their home for ever. She felt his hand placed gently on her head. Then sensing her intention of following him he stopped her by raising his hand.

Do you remember what you told me on the banks of the Vaitarna? he asked. Yes, she replied hesitantly. Seeing that he wanted her to continue she proceeded. I said: I will not let you go alone my Baba. I would gladly follow you to where you go. *But you said something more*, he insisted. You said: *but my time has not yet come. It is now as it was then. Your time has not yet come. Your role now is to stay by our son.* In the ensuing panic she screamed: Come back my Baba, come back, to me, I am alone. She was holding out her hands towards him pleadingly. *Maya* he replied calmly: *why do you think I am going?* Then she saw the door opening and closing softly behind him. At that moment she woke up perspiring copiously and in the throes of a great agitation. She spent the rest of her night trying desperately to overcome her emotions.

Chapter 29

The Curtain Falls

Early the next morning a sleepless and restless looking woman and her little boy turned towards the *ghat* on their way to school to perform a daily ritual. Their eyes were fixed on the spot where Ganga baba habitually sat staring at the river. But he was not there. They anxiously scrutinized the surrounding trying desperately to locate his whereabouts. No, he was not to be seen. Trying to control her panic the woman asked the sellers standing behind their trolleys whether they had seen Ganga baba that morning. 'No' was their concerned reply. The woman took her son to school and retraced her steps to the *ghat*. She moved to the water's edge and let her eyes wander along the banks as far as her view would carry. There was no trace of him. She wandered listlessly in the direction of the river's flow lost in her dream of that night. Then the time came to fetch her son back from school. That night the two tried to console each other with the thought that the lost *sadhu* would be at his regular seat the next day. But the next day yielded nothing as well. Their concern grew from anxiety to panic and from panic to despondency. Their nights were sleepless.

Then while going to school, two days after, they heard a few people mention a dead body that had been found floating on the river several kilometers downstream and which the people of the place were preparing for a hasty cremation. The idea of school left their minds as they retraced their steps in the direction the people had mentioned. They ran breathing heavily as apprehension and despair gripped their minds and bodies. Then on the sandy banks of the Ganges they saw a makeshift pyre with heaped up wood that had seemingly been gathered hastily from the adjacent forest. The pyre had been ignited and people were fanning the emerging flames. They ran as if letting their legs carry them to the place. Panting heavily they approached the pyre with fear and trepidation. The body of the deceased was fully covered under the pile of wood; just his feet were jutting out. They looked at those lifeless feet, and recognized him. The two oval birthmarks on the instep of each foot revealed the identity of the 'unknown' old man. The woman pulled her son towards her and held him in a tight embrace. The boy wound his arms around her legs. Their tears flowed freely.

The fire crackled and flared up. The pyre was fully ignited and the dry wood burned lustily. The men sat around it asking themselves the inevitable questions about the identity of the deceased. At a certain distance behind them, squatting and huddled together were a mother and her little son. The mother was covering her face behind the sari held up as a veil uttering distractedly amidst her tears: *baba... my baba*. The little boy was using his mother's body as a niche to hide his own. His sobbing was heart-rending. His grief he expressed with one poignant word which made every other superfluous. He cried out: '*papa*'.

That night a thoroughly distraught and grieving woman lay on the floor with her son cuddled against her, his arms around her waist. She was engrossed in her thoughts thinking of all that had transpired between her and Ganga Baba. And now he was gone. As she dozed off through sheer fatigue, she saw him before her. My baba, she cried out in an upsurge of joy. You have come back to me. *I have come to leave you my spiritual testament, my only possession. On the last night that I visited you, you screamed in panic: Come back my Baba, come back to me. To come back I must go. But where am I to go? I am here, Maya, I am here*. Baba she cried out feeling a great sense of relief. Do you remember the song I sang to you while I was still your student? He nodded affirmatively and he waited as if inviting her to sing it for him once more. She obliged and sang with fervour, her eyes closed and tears flowing down her cheeks:

I'll walk beside you through the world today
While dreams and songs and flowers bless your way
I'll look into your eyes and hold your hand

I'll walk beside you through the golden land
I'll walk beside you through the world tonight
Beneath the starry skies ablaze with light
Within your soul love's tender words I'll hide
I'll walk beside you through the eventide

I'll walk beside you through the passing years
Through days of cloud and sunshine, joys and tears
And when the great call comes, the sunset gleams
I'll walk beside you to the land of dreams

And in that moment, time dissolved. She realized that not only had nothing changed but that nothing would change, that they were all fixed in an eternal present, an eternal here and now. The singer was the same, the song as well and so also the listener. Where were the several decades of distance that separated the two in time and space? Both had been obliterated in the twinkling of an eyelid. Time had revealed to her its real face, that of illusion. When she opened her eyes, he was still there. *Do you remember what I once told you my baba*? she was now asking him. I said: *You are going no where, you are staying where you are. Yes, my baba, there is no where you can go. You are with us: you are HERE.*

When sleep finally overwhelmed her she saw him seated between her and Neelkanth: between joy and its fruit. She was listening to him singing a verse he used to intone as a young teacher:

So deep is the night, no moon tonight
On broken wings, my soul hath taken flight
And left a dream

Their life had been a story, salvaged as anonymous treasure from the ocean of story: it had been a dream. *Neelkanth, Neelkanth,* she muttered as her eyelids succumbed to their weight, her hands groping to feel the presence of her little boy: *you are our story, the story of a dream.*

End